Memoir of Vietnam

1967

Memoir of Vietnam

1967

BY

WILLIAM S. FEE

LITTLE MIAMI PUBLISHING CO.
MILFORD, OHIO
2015

Little Miami Publishing Co.
P.O. Box 588
Milford, Ohio 45150-0588
www.littlemiamibooks.com

Copyright ©2015 by William S. Fee. All rights reserved. No part of this book may be reproduced or transmitted in any form or by any means, electronic or mechanical, including photocopying, recording or by any information storage and retrieval system without written permission from the author, except for the inclusion of brief quotations in a review.

Printed in the United States of America on acid-free paper.

ISBN-13: 978-1-941083-04-8

Library of Congress Control Number: 2015942402

Dedicated to Sally, my wife of forty four years, who stood by me through the dark days of my life.

And to the men of Delta Company, First Battalion, Eighteenth Regiment, First Infantry Division. We are brothers forever.

Contents

	Preface **ix**
	Introduction **1**
Chapter 1	First Impressions **9**
Chapter 2	Friendships **17**
Chapter 3	Hardships **27**
Chapter 4	Combat **41**
Chapter 5	Aftermath **85**
Chapter 6	Coping with Vietnam **97**
Appendix	Letters Home **109**
	Index **117**
	About the Author **121**

Preface

NOT MANY ACCOUNTS REGARDING THE WAR IN VIETNAM, personal or historical, have a happy ending. While I would not characterize these memoirs in such a light, the process of updating my experiences from the war have provided me with a degree of closure, even satisfaction, which had been missing since I first undertook this task. I began writing these memoirs while still a patient at the army hospital in Valley Forge, Pennsylvania. Following the night I was wounded and evacuated from the war zone on November 1, 1967, my subsequent hospitalization lasted more than ten months. Upon my discharge from the army in September 1968, I typed the words of the first edition and placed the manuscript on a shelf, which sat there unread for more than forty years.

I have been greatly blessed with the good fortune of remaining in contact with many of my buddies from Delta Company,

1st Battalion, 18th Regiment, First Infantry Division. No greater friendships exist than those forged under hostile fire, when one's life depends upon the soldiers next to you, some of whom never came home, and when the common bond of combat weaves together the hearts and minds of a small group of veterans.

Since they were written in 1968, my memoirs remained incomplete throughout the years of the 1970s, 80s and 90s. I have been blessed with continued friendships of a small group of veterans from Delta Company, including General Richard Cavazos (retired), who led the 1st Battalion as a lieutenant colonel in the summer and fall of 1967. Even though the bonds of our brotherhood were seeded in Vietnam, a small group of us met for the first time since the war in 1985, and we have maintained friendships and reunions to this day.

The manuscript of the introduction and first four chapters largely remain untouched from 1968, when I was a twenty-year-old soldier recuperating at Valley Forge. Our reunions, phones calls, letters, and friendships, however, have allowed for further introspection about our year in Vietnam (for me, just four months), and the final two chapters include information learned from our gatherings, particularly the enemy we were fighting, and how middle age has enriched our love for one another.

The hard years for us were the 1970s, when most of us were adrift in a sea of hostility, indifference, and loneliness. Those were bad years to be a Vietnam veteran. Few of our marriages survived that decade. The accounting of difficulties, and the long journey back to mental and physical health, are as integral to the story of the Vietnam veteran, as the horrors of war themselves.

Updating this book has been a catharsis for me, and has provided the opportunity to share the joys of growing old, cherishing memories of the valor, sacrifice, and sufferings that a small group of young men displayed on a field of battle many years ago. Yes, it is a happy ending for those of us still blessed with life and, for me, having overcome years of depression and isolation, necessitating rebuilding my life with Sally in the late 1970s, and leading a productive and fulfilling life as husband, father, and grandfather.

Bill Fee
November 2013

Introduction

"longing to be a soldier"

THERE COMES A TIME IN EVERYONE'S LIFE when one goes through an experience, large or small, and evolves into a different person. Such an experience may be for just a brief moment, or a course of years; the amount of time is irrelevant, and what one achieves and learns through a life-changing experience is just as variable. These few short pages will walk you through an experience which transformed my life, my outlook on life, and my will to live each day to the fullest. The setting is War Zone C in the former South Vietnam, from just north of Saigon up to the Cambodian border. The time was summer and fall 1967. My assignment was rifleman with Delta Company, First Battalion, 18th Infantry Regiment, First Infantry Division, nicknamed the "Swamp Rats." This story was not written to add historical context to the Vietnam War, nor did I attempt to purposefully expose my personal feelings about the war's controversial aspects at that time. This simply is a story about the life of an infantryman in Vietnam in the early stages of the war, when public support at home was still strong, but the war was not yet in the daily newspaper headlines, nor leading the network evening newscasts. The following pages describe the life of an ordinary combat infantry soldier, which bred hardships, mental strains, pain, fear, and yet, lasting friendships among those who were fortunate enough to come home.

Up to nineteen years of age, my life was comfortable, my family was nurturing, and I lacked nothing. I was brought up in a middle class, humble environment, with loving parents and one older brother. Life was easy, and as a sophomore at the University of Cincinnati, I should have been focused on my studies, girlfriends, fraternity, and parties—the sustenance of college life in the 1960s. My grades were average—not good, but satisfactory enough to keep me enrolled in school, and exempted from the draft.

This story begins in the fall of 1966, as I started my second year in college. News of the war had begun to become more prominent, yet had not reached the crescendo level of prominence it would achieve following the Tet Offensive in January 1968. Protests against the war began to spread in the streets and college campuses, but in 1966 there still remained a majority support for the war. I grew more aware and interested in this war as the headlines more frequently featured the events in Southeast Asia. Juxtaposed with the growing conflict on the battlefields of Vietnam was my life on the campus at the University of Cincinnati, dominated by classes, dating, fraternity parties, hazing, and plenty of beer. Absent from this scene were discussions about the war, the tragic loss of life on both sides of the conflict, and the justification for our growing presence and sacrifice in Southeast Asia.

One particular Friday night in October 1966, I found myself at a fraternity party in a VFW Hall just off campus, with the sound of bands blazing, beer flowing, and the usual debauchery of college life on the weekends. I remember leaning against the wall, gazing at the surroundings, saying to myself that no one at the party cared at all about the sacrifices being made by a still small group of American soldiers, halfway around the world, who were caught up in a distant, unpopular war. I felt it was hugely unjust that the sacrifice of these soldiers was disregarded by the press, forgotten by the public, ultimately deemed too unimportant to be debated. At least those who protested against the war had an opinion, and cared. I faced two realities at this time in my life—the inanity of my surroundings, versus the suffering and sacrifice of young men in the Vietnam War. As my interest in course work at the University of Cincinnati waned, I became more and more focused on the war, often having to meander a few pages into the newspaper before finding a story about it. That fall *Time Magazine* featured a poignant picture of an infantry platoon in combat. I cut it out, and placed it on my desk in my room as a reminder that this war, indeed, was real, and that, somehow, I was connected with it.

As awareness of the war started to grow in the fall of 1966, so did the sporadic protests, debates and news coverage. However, the war's reality, and its toll on the soldiers fighting it, occupied more space in my mind than column inches in the newspapers. I had always appreciated my comforts, and the love which my family openly bestowed on me. I felt I had so much for which to be grateful, and began to feel guilty for not acting upon my instinct, as well as my obligation, especially since so many young men were drafted against their will to fight this war. The paradox of my focus and obsession with Vietnam, and my loss of interest in school, compelled me to make a decision.

In a sense, I felt lonely and alone, and worried about how to share the news with my parents about my sense of obligation to enlist in the army. It was at this time that Sally Isphording entered my life. A sorority sister of a young lady I had doted on all fall, only to be rebuffed in no uncertain terms, Sally tried to soften the blow of the rejection I felt. First, a phone call. Then, a meeting after dinner. Suddenly, we both felt an attraction which we knew to be love, but one which presented immense problems with my intent on enlisting. After all, why would a very attractive young lady throw herself on someone who was going away, into a very uncertain future. Perhaps Sally was the moth to my flame, but our relationship was sealed on those long nights in November and December 1966, as we discussed the pain I felt from longing to be a soldier, but tied to the trivialities of everyday life as a college student. My decision to change my world would devastate my family, alienate my friends, and perhaps end a deepening love Sally and I had developed. Despite this developing relationship, the decision to enlist was cemented in my mind when I looked around and observed the indifference to and ignorance of the war among my friends. Selfishly, in my own mind, I felt that my going over there would make a difference, not the least a statement, to my friends who seemed not to care about the war. Most were dumbfounded, some were angry, about my decision. My parents were heartbroken; in their final attempt to dissuade me from enlisting, they told me they would purchase a grand piano if I changed my mind. This small act of bribery was admirable, and a loving act from fearful parents, and even though I understood and grieved over their fear, I could not change my mind. Sally, torn between her blossoming love and pending separation from the object of that affection, strangely supported my decision. Perhaps that first act of understanding and devotion was the seed for our relationship to come.

I confess that my decision was not purely patriotic. The mind and heart of a nineteen-year-old boy, one who had rarely traveled, and certainly had not seen the world, was prone to the intoxication of a dangerous adventure. Vietnam and the war were abstracts, and the lack of comprehension about the specific sacrifices which would take place allowed me to look at the next year with anticipation and eagerness. I was embarking on an adventure which none of my friends or family members clearly understood; yet once I had signed the papers, I felt at peace. I was part of a larger picture, on the world stage, and a world totally alien to everything I had known. I was excited, afraid, and proud. For once I looked forward to the days ahead, leaving the mundane world of college classes behind.

I entered the service on January 9, 1967. I had enlisted in the army, and volunteered for an MOS (military occupational specialty) in infantry. I also had told the recruiter I was volunteering for duty in Vietnam. I had left little room for misunderstanding. My basic training took place at Fort Knox, and advanced infantry training at Fort Polk, Louisiana. While at Fort Knox, one of the training officers learned of my piano background, and asked me to audition for the army band. Despite my original intention for entering the service, and against my own inclination, I did so. Following the audition, word soon returned that I had qualified for the army band, and would be transferred to Fort Lee, Virginia, for band training, for service in the U.S. Army Band. Once again my world was turned upside down, but I agreed to this change in MOS because I felt there was destiny involved somehow. If the army really needed me to play the piano, perhaps my service to the country would be more fitting and rewarding.

It was not to be. During the last week of basic training, all recruits received their papers for their advanced training, and

Above: Day before enlistment. January 8, 1967.
Below: Last day at home before going to Vietnam. June 1967.

mine read "Fort Polk Infantry Training." Someone in the army had made a mistake, and the records of my audition were lost. Again, my world caved in, and I had to immediately change direction and focus on the days ahead. My family tried to intervene, but there was no changing the orders for advanced infantry training. Perhaps it was better that the army granted no leave to the recruits who graduated from basic training, and boarded us all on a train to Louisiana immediately following graduation. By not returning home to face family and friends, and my dear Sally, I was able to save face, regroup my thoughts, and once again focus on my original goal of serving in Vietnam. I felt ashamed that I had allowed myself to deviate from my intention to fight in the war. The train ride to Louisiana was long, uncomfortable, sleepless, and harsh. I had ample time to think, and reorganize my priorities. God's will, I believed, had played this hand, and I accepted it willingly.

Advanced infantry training at Fort Polk slowly unveiled the world which waited for us in Vietnam. Training was brutally realistic, led by veterans who had returned from Vietnam. Our training ground was located in a section of the Fort affectionately named "Tigerland." As our transport trucks entered and left the grounds, recruits were required to growl like tigers as the trucks passed underneath the Tigerland sign. Final infantry training took place at Fort Lewis, Washington, during the month of June 1967, as we waited for departure to Vietnam. It was at this time that we were informed that we would be serving in the First Infantry Division in Vietnam, one of the most decorated units in the army. (Of course, we wondered aloud if that was good or bad news). One thing was clear at this point—six months into my service—the young men I had trained with at Knox and Polk, and now at Lewis, would be traveling together by ship to Vietnam, and would form as Delta Company in the

First Infantry Division. Up to now, the division had only three rifle companies for each battalion—Alpha, Bravo, and Charlie. As part of the troop buildup of the late 1960s, the addition of a Delta Company would increase the size of the Big Red One battalions by 25 percent. It was not lost on any of us that this presented a huge advantage to us. Most recruits were sent to Vietnam as replacements, one at a time, as soldiers were killed or rotated home following their 365-day tour of service. Replacements found themselves alone, a green recruit among a company of seasoned, sometimes hostile, war weary soldiers. The Delta Company's biggest advantage would be its cohesive force of soldiers who had trained together for six months, and who cared for each others' safety. The downside, of course, was inexperience. How would this entire "green" outfit handle itself in its first firefight? The next few months would answer that question clearly.

On Thursday, June 29, 1967, the members of the new Delta companies of the First Infantry Division boarded the USNS *Geiger* en route to Vung Tau, Vietnam. Sixteen hundred troops, each with one duffel bag, crowded onto the ship, with hammocks stacked six deep in the hold. The ten-thousand-mile voyage would last three weeks, and not a day would go by without the stench of vomit from seasickness covering the deck, the hold and the mess facilities. As the coastline of Tacoma, Washington, sunk below the horizon, my adventure had begun, and the voyage would allow plenty of time to think, read, and prepare for the biggest adventure of my life.

CHAPTER 1

First Impressions

"beginning an adventure of a lifetime"

On July 21, 1967, we reached the shores of South Vietnam. I had spent twenty-three days at sea, aboard the troop carrier ship USNS *Geiger*. We landed at the port of Vung Tau, south of Saigon, in the late afternoon, and were extremely disappointed to hear that we could not disembark. Too late in the day, with too little time to assemble truck convoys to our new homes, we were told. We were now in a war zone, and could not travel at night.

I did not sleep my first night in Vietnam. As we lay in our hammocks, we could hear depth charges exploding in the harbor—a defensive maneuver to keep Viet Cong sackers from detonating an explosive device against the hull of the ship. *Welcome to Vietnam,* I mumbled to myself. At 0700 hours in the morning we assembled on deck, claimed our duffel bags, and walked ashore to the sound of patriotic pieces played by an army band. Fine coincidence, I thought, as I tried to keep my senses straight and soak in the strange new sights of my new home for the next twelve months. Since it was seven o'clock in the morning in Vietnam, it would be seven o'clock the night before at home, which made the distance and separation from home even more unbearable.

It was strange to set foot on this land, a culmination of months of training, anticipation, and planning. I thought back to the fall of the previous year—1966—and how I seemingly longed to be here; and now, here I was, in the company of my new friends, beginning an adventure of a lifetime. I was

USNS Geiger

thrilled, and fearful, as I stepped in line to board the truck convoy to Di An (pronounced zee-on), where the headquarters for the First Infantry Division in Vietnam was located. The four-hour ride to Di An revealed a beautiful lush landscape of rice paddies and farms, with farmers in the fields with their water buffaloes, and women squatting in the marshes picking or planting rice. There was little talk on the ride as we absorbed the beautiful sights, saturated in sweat from the hot, humid air. As we arrived at Di An, located seventeen miles north of Saigon, we assembled in a part of camp with large tents filled with cots and wooden floors, and moved into the mess building—a plain, wooden building with a cement floor with screened windows and doors. I was with Delta Company, the newest of four rifle companies in the 1st Battalion, 18th Infantry Regiment of the First Division. We took our seats, and some on the floor, as we waited for our battalion commander, Lt. Col. Richard Cavazos, to enter the building and meet with us.

When Colonel Cavazos arrived, I was impressed by his humble stature and appearance. He sat down on a table in the middle of our gathering, introduced himself, and immediately began to give us information for which we had craved for weeks. The colonel informed us that our battalion, the 1st of the 18th, was known as the Swamp Rats, for the campaigns previously conducted in the Rung Sat war zone north of Saigon. His informal, congenial style of discussing the history of our unit was comforting to me, and his demeanor and concentration—I remember that he looked at us in the eyes as he spoke—put us at ease. The one remark I remember vividly, and one we recall to this day when we have our reunions, was when he said "Boys, I will never place you in danger. If there is any doubt about my control of the battle, I will give the order to withdraw, and call in the artillery." Those words would become prophetic in the months ahead. We did not know the stature or background of our new commander, but our short time in Vietnam revealed the depth of his courage, leadership, and how much he cared for "his boys."

What interested me upon our arrival at Di An was the Vietnamese people themselves who were present throughout the camp in various support jobs. I had never been in a foreign country, and hearing a foreign language was new to me, especially one as different as Vietnamese. The dialect seemed jumbled, nonsensical. The Vietnamese were small, quiet, and hard working. We could not communicate with them, so smiles were all we could pass on. I felt uneasy around them at first, they seemed so different and foreign; ironic in that *we* were the foreigners in *their* land. I caught myself staring at them, in the mess hall, where they served the food and cleaned up afterward, but grew accustomed to being among them after several weeks. Soon our Vietnamese friends blended into the landscape around the camp, and we grew used to seeing them wherever we went, as GIs often do in the countries they are serving. Still, the Vietnamese were so different from Americans. I was just a low-ranking PFC (private first class) and so was not exposed to the higher class of citizens in the country—only servants and farmers. These people lived a life of hardship and poverty. Some of the living conditions in Vietnam were abhorrent and appalling, something I had never seen. The Vietnamese (the term "gook" unfortunately would become part of the GI language) would accept anything the Americans gave them, often foraging for treasures out of the garbage dumps around Di An. Favorite items were discarded C ration cans, full of food which was considered a delicacy for them. Although the Vietnamese may have lived in unhealthy conditions, at least to our standards, they were extremely thrifty, and would never waste a drop of food or any other material that was useful to them. They may have been crude in their methods of living, but at least these people appreciated what they had, and rarely wasted a single item in their possession. The Vietnamese also never self indulged in anything except hard work. When on patrol one day near the village of Song Be (pronounced song bay), I gave a little girl a roll of lifesavers. I had never seen a face light up so quickly with happiness and pleasure; she ran into her house as fast as she could, apparently to show her mother, brothers, and sisters the sweet treasure she had been given. The Vietnamese may have lived in filth in the countryside, but this was the only life they knew, and were not ashamed. Americans may have been shocked to see these conditions, dirty in the villages, and so primitive in the country, but this was the reality of Vietnam in the 1960s. When we realized that these people were living in a war-torn country, full of terror and destruction, for over twenty years, we had come to respect and admire their pride. They were the ones who were suffering, with the burden of sacrifice on their shoulders. These people had to live with fear, death, and terror all of their lives. They were tired, exhausted and still afraid and distrusting of Americans. Granted, it was my opinion that the civil war among the South Vietnamese, and those who assisted the Viet Cong, was extending this war, and thus they were bringing it on themselves. Either by force, or free choice, some Vietnamese were compelled to help the Communists; but there were many more people who faced this choice by sacrificing their lives in the daily war against terror and tyranny, the source of their own misery for the last two decades. One could not blame the Vietnamese if they had just given in to the Communists. Many were courageous, and were dedicated to fighting for a life extremely hard to attain—a life of freedom.

From the very start of our tour in Vietnam, we were lectured to, instructed, and indoctrinated that our unit, the "Big Red One," was the finest, proudest, and most historic division in the U.S. Army. It was quite true that the First Infantry Division had a battle record unequaled in the army—from the trenches of World War I, the European theater in the Second World War, and the first to reach the shores of Vietnam in division strength.

The Big Red One had been responsible for more enemy killed up to this time of the war, 1967, and had been decorated for the least casualties suffered than any other combat unit in Vietnam. We were told to wear our Big Red One patch with honor, and we did. We felt proud that we were part of "the best of this man's army," a motto proudly accepted by every unit in the armed forces. However, we indeed understood the value of the combat records of the First Division, and could tell, without bias or prejudice, that we were actually part of the best fighting unit in this distant war. In classes during the day, we also were taught the history of the First Battalion, the Swamp Rats, a record dating back to the War of 1812. We respected Colonel Cavazos from the start; he seemed one of us, an average Joe, and was congenial and down to earth, unlike most of the other officers we had come to know. It was clear from the beginning that Cavazos was a "soldier's soldier," and he intended to lead the men of Delta Company from the ground, close to the combat, which would make it easy for us to respect and follow him. Much more about this wonderful man, and his style of leadership, later in the story.

Cavazos told us that the rest of the battalion—Alpha, Bravo, and Charlie Companies—were out in the field, a term meaning they were on a combat operation, or were on search patrols somewhere in War Zone C. Even though all of us had completed eight weeks of basic training, another eight weeks of advanced infantry training at Fort Polk, and four weeks of Vietnam training at Fort Lewis, the colonel told us we would undergo another six weeks of training, in the area around Di An, before we would be dispatched to the field. At first I was greatly disappointed; it was now July, and I had spent seven months in training, and now that we were in the country, I had hoped we could join the battalion right away. It was not to be. However, Colonel

Cavazos informed us there was much to learn about the First Division—its tactical maneuvers and the terrain in War Zone C, the combat area between Saigon and the Cambodian border to the north, which represented our area of operations. Training would take place in the field surrounding Di An, which was a relatively safe area, and consequently, should be removed from combat.

So, my year in Vietnam had finally begun. We were all made to feel as much at home as possible. Our company area had a nice wooden mess area with a concrete floor and our tents for sleeping—complete with wooden planks for walkways, and mosquito nets on the cots. The tents slept up to twelve soldiers, enough for one squad (ten men at full force). Each squad had a couple of NCOs (noncommissioned officers) who had been in-country for a while, and had experienced combat. These men would live with us, and serve as our trainers for the next six weeks. Plans were that when we finished training, they would be our squad leaders in combat. Although I had my twelve months still ahead, I wasn't feeling too bad nor anxious. Curious, yes, about the adventure for which I had anticipated for so long, going back to my college days nine months earlier. I was about to set out on a journey which was to become completely different than anything I had known in my twenty years of life. I was anxious about what the next year would bring, not knowing that my stay in Vietnam would be an abbreviated one, and that the next four months would make an impression on me which would change my outlook on life forever.

CHAPTER 2

Friendships

"We had each other"

Our training started immediately with the assignment of platoons and squads, issuing and firing of weapons, classes, and a repeat of our training stateside. We essentially covered the same classes as we had at Fort Polk, although the sounds of artillery firing throughout the day, a precautionary measure for protection of the camp perimeter, and the noises of helicopters and planes landing on the airstrip, heightened our senses and made us realize that, unlike the swamps of Louisiana, we were now in a war zone. As the weeks progressed, we would patrol more and more outside the perimeter of Di An, in "no man's land," to learn how to dig the First Division's style of foxhole, and adapt to life in the field. Training was interesting, and very actual, so we were kept busy, which made the time fly by. Although the days were filled with nonstop activity, never did I feel that it didn't bother me to be away from home. There I was, halfway around the world, ten thousand miles from home, so yes, I was homesick. The twelve-hour time difference made it worse. I would get up in the morning around six o'clock, and think of my family just then eating dinner the night before. It was hard to imagine this distance and separation, and made me feel like I was in a different world altogether.

Although I felt loneliness, I was not alone, for in that far away country there were over a half million men and women who felt as I did. I grew very close to the men around me. Except for the officers and a few sergeants, all of us were young, with the average age around twenty. My squad leader, a young buck sergeant (a three striper) was named Steve Pritchett, and he was even younger than I. Since the rifle squads ate, slept, trained, and played together, the men in each squad became as close as brothers. We had a real fine group of men in our squad, and we came to know each other very quickly during the months of July and August of 1967.

George Adams was my first squad leader. He was an African American from Virginia, and had a distinctly Virginian drawl in his speech. Adams was the most serious minded of the NCOs, because he had been in-country the longest. He would joke and play around when we were at ease, but in the field during the day, he was strict as any squad leader could be. We all made fun of his southern accent. Later on, in October, he would be promoted to platoon sergeant, and Steve Pritchett would assume command of the squad. Pritch, as we called him, was the opposite of Adams; he was fun loving, joking, and always cracking one liners. He talked incessantly about his home state of California, and his handful of girlfriends. Pritch was not prone to taking anyone seriously, but this never prevented him to becoming very close friends with a handful of the soldiers who served with him, including me. While at Di An, he left for a two-week stay at headquarters as a desk clerk for the Red Cross. For a while, there was a possibility that he would remain there permanently for rest of his tour in Vietnam. Lucky for us, but not for him, Pritch rejoined our squad just before we were to go into the field for the first time and join the rest of the battalion. He was disappointed, naturally, at losing a comfy desk job with three hot meals and showers every day; but privately, he admitted that it felt good to be back with his friends, and he even confessed that he was lonely at the Red Cross. Apparently my feelings for the squad were mirrored by Pritch, thus accounting for the closeness of our friendship.

Also in our squad were Shelby Davidson and Mike Ciliberti, our grenadiers; Steve Diehl and Jack Freppon, who carried automatic weapons (an older rifle than the M-16, the M-14 had a wooden base, and was retrofitted to fire as an automatic weapon); and finally, Frank Fierro and Pete Haymon, who rounded out the riflemen in the squad. These men were my clos-

Mike Ciliberti, Bill Fee, Steve Pritchett, Frank Fierro.
August 31, 1967, Di An, Vietnam.

est friends in Vietnam. We slept, ate, trained, fought, and cared for each other very much. Little did I realize at that time that some of these friends would be with me for a lifetime, and some would be dead before their combat service in Vietnam would be completed.

The closeness of our friendship revealed itself in some unique ways. Jack Freppon came from Cincinnati, although we did not meet until we assembled in Di An after we arrived in country. He attended the University of Cincinnati, as did I, dropped out of school to enlist in the army in January 1967, and volunteered for infantry and Vietnam service. How we did not meet until Di An remains a mystery, but our friendship was special from the beginning. Both Diehl and Ciliberti had girlfriends who were nurses, as was my Sally. Wives and girlfriends probably consumed about 95 percent of the conversations we had whenever we talked of home.

Frank Fierro was the quiet one. He worked extremely hard at any task given him—silently, obediently, completely. In the field, when an infantry battalion digs in for the night, after the foxholes are dug, the soldiers set out an intricate array of trip flares around the perimeter, and in combat situations the flares are accompanied with claymore mines, which can be triggered electronically to explode as the enemy nears the perimeter. Fierro was the master of night defenses; his work was an art, and his ability to leave no square foot of territory in front of his foxhole uncovered was uncanny. In combat, one learns to stay near to a man like Frank Fierro. Surely, I did.

Mike Ciliberti was the staunch Catholic, and never hesitated to remind the rest of the squad that he was going to heaven, and us to hell, because we were Protestants, mostly in jest, fortunately. His faith kept him from yelling obscenities, pushed him to recite prayer before meals and bedtime, and we frequently found him reading the Bible. When I was with Ciliberti, I did not feel the least bit bothered by reading Perry Mason novels, by Erle Stanley Gardner, which Sally's mother frequently sent in her care boxes.

Standing: George Adams (Squad Leader), Steve Diehl, Bill Fee, Steve Pritchett. Kneeling is Mike Ciliberti.

Steve Diehl was the All-American prep high school football star—clean cut and clean living—with a couple of years of college under his belt before he was drafted. His job in the squad, besides carrying an automatic rifle, was to serve as point man on patrols. Few positions in Vietnam were more dangerous than walking point. Diehl had the responsibility of leading the patrol, usually a company-sized group of soldiers, using his compass and map. Terrain in Vietnam was tough, tight, and dense. Diehl had to cut away the vines and brush with a machete when on patrol, while keeping his eyes fixed on trees, bushes, and any sign of the enemy laying in wait for an ambush. Everyone respected Diehl for his toughness, humor and his ability to leave it all behind back in the foxhole, as we talked of girlfriends and life at home.

Among all the soldiers with whom I served in Vietnam, I spent most of my down time with Steve Pritchett and Jack Freppon. Jack and I frequently engaged in conversation about home—Cincinnati, our families, fun things to do there, and familiar subjects like the Reds and the University of Cincinnati. In late October 1967, when our First Infantry Division battalion encountered the heaviest fighting we had seen to date, following an exhausting battle which lasted all afternoon, I remember Jack and I shaking hands back in our foxhole, promising that following our tour in Vietnam, we would visit each other's homes in Cincinnati, meet our families, and start a new life together as friends and civilians. It was not to be, for Jack would become one of my good buddies lost to the war.

As we went through training in August and early September of 1967, and the inevitability of combat grew closer, so did our friendships. Nights at Di An were usually free time for us; we'd take in a movie, play cards, sit around the cots and sing, or go to the club for some beers. That was my routine the first six weeks in Vietnam—patrol by day, attend classes on First Division tactics, learn how to build a Big Red One foxhole, relax at night, write a few letters, and get about six hours sleep. Not bad for time which counted against my 365 days in country. Our training taught us how to fight as a team, one solid unit, instead of individuals. Crucial lessons for combat. Our platoon sergeant, Sergeant Page, lectured us one day that a group of individuals in combat will not succeed; we had to fight as a cohesive team to fulfill our duty—be alert, watch out for your buddy, stay alive and kill the enemy. I don't think these words resonated with us at Di An. Everything we had learned in our stateside training, and so far at Di An, was preparing for battle, not actually experiencing the terror of the moment itself. At target practice, we shot at pop-up targets; and yet we were approaching the moment when those targets would be human beings, who would be desperately trying to kill me. I took Sergeant Page's advice very seriously.

One night at Di An, after dinner, as I was sitting around our tent, when I received orders to report to the chapel. I hadn't the slightest idea why the division chaplain wanted to see me. When I arrived at the chapel, he told me that he learned from reading my military records that I played the piano, an obvious reference to my disappointment at Fort Knox. He asked that I attend Sunday morning services at the chapel to play the piano for the services. His chaplain assistant had just DEROSed home (Date Eligible to Return from Over Seas), and the chaplain needed someone to play the piano for Sunday morning services. The request hit me like a ton of bricks. I felt like a yoyo; I had originally enlisted in the army to fight in Vietnam. In basic training I had the opportunity to change my MOS (military occupational specialty) from infantry to music, and went for it, only to be disappointed. I was now in Southeast Asia, and happy to be there, with a group of young men with whom I had trained for months. And now this, another dangling carrot to tease me with the chance to play the piano. In confiding to the chaplain, he told me I could fulfill this duty on a temporary basis until a new chaplain assistant arrives, and besides, why not come to the chapel in the evening and practice the piano all I want, he asked? This was a perfect solution. For the weeks spent at Di An in training, I frequently walked to the chapel in the evening and practiced my heart out; all of my favorites—Chopin, Rachmaninoff, Liszt—amazingly streamed forth, even though I had no music, and it had been eight months since I sat at a piano.

Sunday mornings allowed me to get back into the practice of attending church as well, so this development was certainly a satisfying one for me personally.

September came all too suddenly with news that Delta Company was to join the rest of the battalion in the field. We had been at Di An for almost eight weeks, trained hard, learned new tactics, grown closer together, and were ready to demonstrate our skills as a fighting team. I walked to the chapel to visit the chaplain to give him the news, and say goodbye. Counter to what he had said a few weeks prior, he asked me to stay with him as his new chaplain assistant, replying that he could take care of the necessary paperwork to change my MOS. My response was immediate, yet humbly grateful. No, I said, I had come this far, I had fulfilled my original destiny to join the fight in Vietnam, and especially after having been with Delta Company the last eight weeks, I was not about to leave my friends. I remember the surprised look on the chaplain's face, and my own personal satisfaction with my response. Pritch told us, when he returned from the Red Cross, how lonely he was while he was gone. I knew that if I stayed, I would regret the decision.

End of my training at Di An, September 1967.

I slept well that night, unaware of the degree of peril and danger which was ahead for the boys of Company D, 1/18th, First Infantry Division.

Our training had accomplished its purpose. By early September we had learned to act and fight as an infantry company. Indeed, we felt like brothers, and were not shy with each other about our need to stay close and look out for each other. Pritch was my closest friend; an excellent soldier who had already experienced combat, and was soon to return to the field for more as one of our NCOs (noncommissioned officers, mostly sergeants). So many of our nights at Di An were spent together at the club, at the mess hall, or just sitting on a bunk in our tent talking. The friendship I had with Pritch, and the other members of my rifle squad, would play an immense role in the weeks ahead, especially in combat. To know your buddies in the foxhole next to you was to place faith in them, as they did in me. Months of training together in the States, and eight more weeks at Di An, and we were ready. The rest of the battalion—Companies Alpha, Bravo, and Charlie—were waiting for us at Quon Loi, an hour north of Di An near the Cambodian border. The men of Delta Company felt we were prepared; certainly we were anxious about the months ahead. We had each other, and that made us feel safe, secure, but still a little wary about the hard days to come.

CHAPTER 3

Hardships

"I realized how far I was from home"

THE DAY WE WERE WAITING FOR FINALLY CAME on September 13, 1967. Delta Company was ordered to fly up and join the rest of the battalion at Quon Loi, approximately sixty miles north of Di An. We were informed that this sector was a secure, noncombat zone, yet excitement and curiosity rose in the ranks. We were thrilled to finally arrive in the field, to take part in operations with the other companies, and show what we had learned at Di An. Most of all, we wanted to impress Colonel Cavazos. Our time in and exposure to Vietnam had been confined to Di An, and now were would be flying and patrolling throughout the area of War Zone C called the Iron Triangle, the stretch of land north of Saigon up to the Cambodian border, which included a dangerous part of the country where the Ho Chi Minh Trail entered South Vietnam.

On the morning of September 13 we rode in a truck convoy

from Di An to Bien Hoa, where one of the busiest military airports in the country was located. The ride afforded us our first view of the countryside outside Di An, and I was captivated by the busy streets, scooters, and the South Vietnamese themselves. Arriving at Bien Hoa, we had a two-hour wait for our transport planes to arrive. Sitting there on the tarmac, we witnessed a group of soldiers from the First Infantry Division boarding a plane—destination, home. Stateside. The land of the big PX. These men had spent twelve months in South Vietnam, and it was hard for me to imagine that I was still in college when they arrived the previous year. I remembered how I longed to be part of this war, wanted to witness the event of my generation, and now I was here. Seeing these men board the plane gave me hope that next June would come fast. We saw some soldiers arriving at Bien Hoa as well, their first day in country. The scene of both groups of soldiers was as heartbreaking as it was exhilarating, and made me feel part of history. I had no regrets.

Before we knew it, we were loaded onto several C-130 military transport planes, packed like sardines, and into the air. The C-130s were the mainstay of troop transports in the war. The four-engine turboprop was fast and maneuverable. We were on the ground at Quon Loi within thirty minutes.

Quon Loi was an insignificant outpost high on a hill, surrounded by miles of rubber tree plantations in all directions. The plantations were owned mostly by wealthy French families, a holdover from the French colonial days prior to their defeat at Dien Bien Phu in 1954, and were cultivated and managed by South Vietnamese farmers. Sap from the rubber trees was processed in a similar fashion to maple syrup; the bark was cut in a downward spiral, and the sticky white sap would flow down the indentation into a porcelain bowl at the bottom of the tree. From any point at the Quon Loi outpost I could see nothing but rubber trees, neatly lined in rows for miles, with a three- or four-foot trench dug parallel to the trees in every other row. The trenches were used for irrigation in the wet months (summer), and had to last during the dry, hot winter season. The outpost was basically an airstrip on top of a mountain, and our battalion foxholes formed a perimeter around the landing zone. An artillery battery was positioned on the north end of the airstrip. As U.S. troops patrolled around the hills and valleys surrounding Quon Loi, the artillery would serve as reinforcement cover if an enemy force was encountered. With the Cambodian border about ten miles to the north, the area held strategic importance to combating the movement of North Vietnamese and Viet Cong forces as they entered the country from the north. Yet for now the area was quiet.

Our first responsibility in the field was reconnaissance patrols, which included six- to eight-hour daily hikes up and down the hills in search for the enemy. After a few days the routine became boring yet exhausting, and we learned quickly that no danger lurked in the rubber tree plantations for Delta Company. The climate of Vietnam from April to November was called the monsoon season, and for good reason. Hard, pouring rain was a daily occurrence, often several times a day, followed immediately afterward by clearing skies and sunshine, resulting in unbearable heat and humidity.

Same at night, a manic-depressive meteorological nightmare. It was absolutely impossible for a soldier to stay dry in the field. Rain would soak us to the bone, creep into the clothes in our backpacks, and down the barrel of our M-16s. Everything I owned was wet, save for my packet of writing paper and pen, which I meticulously wrapped every day in a plastic bag, and nestled deep in my backpack.

When it rained at night, despite the time of year, I could not keep warm. Some of the coldest and most uncomfortable nights of my life were spent during September and October of 1967 in a rain-soaked foxhole.

One night, in particular, illustrated the hardship of an infantry soldier in Vietnam. It was October 1, and Delta Company had been airlifted into a hot LZ (hot landing zone, meaning enemy had been sighted in the area) as part of an operation called Shenandoah. We landed around three o'clock in the afternoon and, after hiking to our night defensive perimeter, we began digging our foxholes at dusk. The process of three hundred men digging holes in a circle, clearing the brush in front of the holes to secure firing lines, fortifying the holes by placing sand bags around the foxhole, and on steel rods above the hole to form a roof, lasted until one o'clock in the morning. We were exhausted from hiking, had no time for dinner, were worried about being attacked, all made worse by a constant downpour which started at dusk. We were wet, hungry, and tired. I was allowed to get first shift for sleep, while some of my buddies took first watch. I had two hours to catch some sleep, and immediately lay down in the wet mud, pulled my poncho over my head and closed my eyes. I was lying prone in two inches of water, completely soaked to the bone, shivering from the cold. But sleep I did. I recall saying to myself that this would be a night I would remember, and it was.

The monsoon rain made it easier for us to stay clean, and cooled the hot summer sun. What it also brought out was the mud of South Vietnam. In Quon Loi, the mud was dark red, heavy, and sticky. It got into everything, from clothes to food to weapons. An infantry soldier on patrol cannot avoid the mud; if a mud hole lay in the path of a patrol, we went through it, as we did one day on patrol. A huge swamp lay directly ahead of our squad, as we were on point for the company-sized reconnaissance patrol. Approximately fifty meters in length, it took our squad over an hour to cross. It came up to our waist, making it terribly difficult to walk through. We had to raise our weapons over our heads as we crossed. It was so thick that as we approached the far side of the swamp, each soldier had to help the man behind him get out, by pulling his weapon. When we were through, we discussed how severely trapped we were by the elements, and would have made easy targets for an ambush had the enemy been in the area.

Life in the field was rough, but so was the soldier. Despite the elements, we had to persevere and be guarded at all times, twenty-four hours a day. In a three-man foxhole, one is always on guard duty, watching and listening intently for the slightest movement or sound. After a patrol—which averaged about ten kilometers during the day, through rugged, dense terrain—upon returning to the NDP (night defensive perimeter, a circle of foxholes with about three hundred men) we would clean our weapons, wash our bodies, and clothes, put on some dry socks, and, if time allowed, write our sweetheart or read a letter from home. We suffered from exhaustion, yet were not able to overcome it with adequate sleep. There is a saying that the U.S. soldier owned the daytime, and Charlie owned the night. Charlie was the enemy, affectionately named after Victor Charlie, or the Viet Cong. An average night's sleep lasted four or five hours, if we were lucky, because everyone took turns on guard duty. The following morning, the same routine of patrolling took place. A 24/7 job.

The harsh climate and exhaustive work resulted in another hardship for the infantry soldier in Vietnam—weight loss. I lost thirty pounds from September to November, and was down to 120 pounds. It was not all due to loss of appetite, although that was the main reason. Sometimes there was no time to eat. In a combat zone, if the luxury of a meal afforded itself, it consisted of C rations—cold meals out of a can lacking any taste and nutrition. In noncombat zones we sometimes were treated to hot meals flown in from Di An, yet that exercise was costly and logistically challenging, so C rations were our main meals. Lack of sustenance was remedied when "care packages" from home would make it to the field. My future mother-in-law, Jean Isphording, was a master of these surprises—shoe boxes filled with luxuries like chocolate, dry socks, Erle Stanley Gardner Perry Mason novels, Kool-Aid for our canteens, and assortments of candy, which were always shared with the rest of squad.

Americans too easily take things for granted, until they are removed from their present circumstances and have to live without the usual comforts of home. I certainly did. I missed hot meals, dry socks, a roof over my head, friends, family, and a life of leisure. On cold rainy nights, knee deep in mud and water in my foxhole, I realized how far I was from home—the extreme opposite of everything I knew and had at home. I used to love hearing the sound and smell of rain falling on the roof of my home or car, but it is quite different when the rain hits your helmet, drips down your face, underneath your clothes, completely soaking your body. Rainy nights were extremely cold and uncomfortable. During these difficult situations, my thoughts often drifted to home, and those comforts I no longer had, and missed so much. Even though I had lost most of my appetite, I would torture myself with the thought of my mother's meatloaf, beef stroganoff, or cherry pie. On hot, humid days in Vietnam, we could only quench our thirst with a canteen of lukewarm water; the best I could do was add a packet of Kool-Aid, which helped to improve the taste, but that was all. Life in the field was devoid of soft drinks, hot food, and dry clothes, the thought of which never left the mind of the combat infantry soldier. In such a short period of time, I grew to appreciate the distance to which I had removed myself from the trivial comforts of home, which now had become luxuries, and mere figments of my imagination.

During the monsoon season—the months of summer and fall—nothing stayed dry. The rain was so hard it would penetrate the backpacks, our belongings, and our bodies to the bone. It took only a few weeks for us to become accustomed to being wet all the time; wet clothes were as common as the leeches that clung to them. We lived with only one extra pair of socks and jungle fatigues in our backpack.

Steve Pritchett and Bill Fee at Quon Loi.

In the field, if they were torn, bloody or wet, we waited a week or more before a resupply helicopter would bring us dry clothes. Imagine wearing the same clothes on your body for a week, no matter how dirty or bloody they became. Now imagine not washing the body in your clothes for a week as well. This is the reason the monsoon rain was welcomed. It cleansed our clothes and our bodies daily, and as soon as the rain stopped, out came the sun and humidity.

We had many companions on patrol in the day, and in our foxholes at night, which served as daily reminders of our circumstance, and contributed to the hardship of life in the field. One family of indigenous little creatures which made life miserable for us were the leeches that always found their way to our skin. The jungle was filled with them, and patrolling through rice paddies, swamps, and rivers during the day allowed them to feast on our bodies, usually without our noticing their attack on our skin. The only way to rid this pest was to poke their skin with a lit cigarette, or a douse of field-issue mosquito repellent. To pluck one from your body would in most cases result in one portion of the leech's head remaining attached. Fire and mosquito repellent always did the trick. Routine duty when returning to our foxholes in the late afternoon following an exhausting patrol included cleaning our weapons and checking the bodies of our buddies for our daytime friends.

At night, our companions were red fire ants, and although they were not as widespread as the leech, if our foxhole was near one of their nests, they would roam everywhere around us at night, biting anything in their way. There was no method to rid ourselves of this nocturnal pest. That's why they became our night time friends in the field. Lucky us.

The best way to escape the hardships and discomfort in the field was talking about home—our family, girlfriends, the food we missed, tall tales of high school triumphs, and memories. This was the first time most of us had been away from home, indeed, in a war half way around the world. Every soldier carried a picture of his girlfriend in his wallet, sealed in clear plastic, cracked and frayed around the edges from constant handling. At any hour of the day I would imagine my girlfriend, Sally, back at home, in nursing classes at the University of Cincinnati, in the dorm at night studying, at the sorority house during the day. The twelve-hour time difference between South Vietnam and Cincinnati made our separation even more distant. Daytime in the jungle was the night before back at home. We all worried about receiving "Dear John" letters, and a couple of the guys in my platoon actually received this bad news. One soldier in particular, Amos Davis, got the bad news in a letter from his wife. They had married only one week before his departure for Vietnam, and she wrote to say she was leaving for another man. Davis was shocked, saddened, and disillusioned, to the point where the Delta Company commander, Capt. Charles Carden, removed him from the field and reassigned him to the rear in Di An as temporary company supply clerk. This demonstrated two things about serving in combat: first a soldier has to be vigilant at all times, and must focus on his duty, be alert to his surroundings, and not be distracted in any way from finding the enemy, and protecting his fellow soldiers. Secondly, the First Infantry Division commanders cared very much for their soldiers, and sending Davis back to the rear protected him from danger, and us as well. Davis was missed, but when we airlifted into the battle of Loc Ninh in late October, he rejoined our platoon for the fight. It was his decision to return to the platoon. Good man, that Amos Davis.

I, too, would think about Sally back at home, knowing that she was free to go out and date (at her mother's insistence!). Sally was a faithful girlfriend, writing letters as often as she could, which was hard considering her busy schedule as a nursing student at the University of Cincinnati. She suffered a tragedy in September, when her father died suddenly from a blood clot. He was only fifty-five years old, and fell off a ladder while painting his house, breaking his hip. He suffered the fatal clot while recuperating in the hospital. When I received the news of his death from Sally, it hit me extremely hard. I had met him only several times before leaving for Vietnam, and I know he was extremely protective of his daughter. I was a young man who entered her life in the fall of 1966, and then left for the service. Any parent in their right mind would tell their child to *move on* and, while Sally dated, she was still my sweetheart. She saved every letter I wrote her while I was away, and they represent an inspiration and testament to our forty-five year relationship. Since Sally's father was not a blood relative, there was no way I could return home for the funeral. The fall of 1967 was a bad time for my future wife; she was having a hard time with grades in school, her father passed away, and in November, the news about me would be another blow for her. Even though I did not have the privilege of knowing Sally's father very well, little did I realize how much he would be with me in the months ahead.

While our battalion was stationed at Quon Loi in September 1967, our days were filled with uneventful, exhausting patrols through the rubber tree plantations, hills, and valleys surrounding the airstrip. Nights were more relaxing, although our squad had to go out on ambush patrol every three nights. Immediately outside the barbed wire perimeter of our foxholes, there were several houses where the local Vietnamese lived. Frequently, some members of our squad received permission to go into the small village, to visit prostitutes. I never understood my buddies' fascination with this practice, nor did I have the desire to do the same. Out of my squad, Freppon, Fierro, Ciliberti, and I were the only ones not to visit the village. Ciliberti was a hardcore Catholic, and said his faith kept him from any desire to spend time with a prostitute. Freppon and I just had better sense, and would rather spend time talking around the foxhole. I was fortunate to have my Sally with me in spirit, and she, too, was an inspiration for my fidelity.

My foxhole partners—Pritchett, Ciliberti, and Fierro —in the field.

Before I enlisted, I often spent time thinking about the war, and my desire to be there. Six months later, I was in Vietnam, and soon would be in combat. Now my thoughts drifted to home, to the dances, classes, and college life that now was so foreign and distant to me. Before, I was on the outside looking in, and now, I was in the middle of it all. Thoughts of home, and Sally, made me lonely, but I knew this year would go by fast, and if I stayed busy, keeping my mind on my duty, and staying alive, my obligation would be over, and I would be able to return to college. That was my plan, and I focused on it continually. My buddies felt the same, in their own way, and talk of my civilian life at home was another bond which brought us closer together. As the weeks passed, our bond grew stronger. One day on patrol at Song Be, Steve Diehl, while serving as point man, suffered a heat stroke. He collapsed, and his body went into convulsions. Diehl was sent to Di An for three days to rehydrate and rest, and since we were in the field, we had no news about his recovery. It was if we had lost a brother, not in combat, but his absence was a big concern for all of us. When he rejoined the squad three days later, we were joyous and relieved.

We had become a cohesive fighting unit—each man depending on the buddy next to him. We were like brothers, and were not afraid to say so. On a three-day break at Phuoc Vinh following several weeks of uneventful search and destroy missions around Quon Loi, I remember standing at the fence along the outer perimeter of the camp, making small talk with some Vietnamese boys from the village. While I was communicating to them in my broken Vietnamese, my squad leader, Sergeant George Adams, an African American from Virginia, approached us, and put his arm around me as he joined the conversation. Two soldiers who had known each other only a couple of months, we were close enough to openly demonstrate an act of brotherhood, and this simple gesture on his part exemplified our relationship—one of closeness and dependence. We wouldn't talk about it, but we all knew just how much we meant to each other. We had to stick out this year together—sleeping, patrolling, eating, and fighting from the same foxhole. Pritch was the cheerleader, and the squad's favorite buddy, and was mostly responsible for keeping us together. If one of us was troubled, hurting, not keeping up with the rest, Pritch would leap into the problem, work with the soldier, and instill a sense of purpose and camaraderie.

Whether it was drinking beer at the club back in Di An, or telling jokes and stories around our foxholes in a safe area, the buddies of the third squad, first platoon of Delta Company were constantly together, like ten brothers in a family. When the day would come to test our training in combat, we felt we would be ready. We all suffered the same hardships and sacrifice, which brought us even closer. However, the real test is combat, and that's what we were there for. This would be the final test, as an individual, and a fighting unit, and the new Delta Company would soon have the opportunity to prove our worth to Colonel Cavazos, as well as entering the history of battle in the Vietnam War.

CHAPTER 4

Combat

"We grew up quickly"

THE DATE WAS OCTOBER 1, 1967. The place was Phuoc Vinh, Vietnam, a base camp for the First Infantry Division, situated in a relatively calm, peaceful part of War Zone C. Delta Company had come here to rest, meaning we had the luxury of cots, tents, showers, hot meals, and, most importantly, sleep; but our weapons were at the ready, and our back packs full, in case we had to move out in a hurry. Even though at rest, we were called a "ready reactionary force," which would allow immediate deployment in case of an emergency. However, this was our first rest in over a month—no patrols, no guard duty, no mud.

When the alert came, we did not believe it at first. Word was given that a Big Red One battalion had been attacked while participating in Operation Shenandoah, in War Zone C only a few miles from Phuoc Vinh. We immediately found ourselves "saddling up," and heading to the helicopter landing zone for a combat air assault. I remember Delta Company walking toward the helicopters, almost in silence, with a few words of encouragement from the sergeants, and to a one, each of us fearing what lie ahead. This would be Delta Company's first test, and while we had yearned and trained for this moment, I was afraid what the day would bring. We were airborne in less than one hour, heading toward a hot landing zone, meaning the enemy was in the area. The chopper rides were always too short, because the scenery below was magnificent, and the calm before the storm was always disconcerting. None of us talked on the way to the LZ—just solitary, anxious thoughts. I thought of some of us not coming home, and wondered to myself who would make it, and who wouldn't. I tried to prepare myself for the battle by imagining who our enemy was, and how the battle would be fought. There was an army reporter on the chopper with us from the *American Traveler* newspaper, the newspaper for the First Infantry Division, and when I discovered his presence, he started asking me some questions. "How do you feel," he asked, and "do you know where we're going?" Up until I had enlisted in the army I had been a spectator of the war, from the comfort of home, looking at the war from the outside in. But now, as I was beginning to taste my first experience of combat, and found myself sitting across from a reporter interviewing me, I had realized the completion of my mission, and felt the distance from home. I was now participating in a war the whole world was watching. I had come a long way, and was embarking on my greatest adventure. An article appeared in the *American Traveler* on October 14, 1967, which included,

> PFC William Fee didn't see any Viet Cong that day, but he and the men of his squad were excited over the news that the 271st Viet Cong Regiment was on the run. Fee, a member of the 1st Battalion, 18th Infantry Regiment,

which acted as a blocking force said, "They told us to hurry up and finish chow, because we were going out in less than half an hour."

As we flew into the LZ (landing zone), we jumped from the helicopter about three feet from the ground; the choppers did not land for fear of an enemy ambush. Immediately we headed for the woodline, just as we were taught in training, and for good reason—we were definitely in a "hot zone," as jets from all directions were dive bombing and strafing near our positions, "loosening up" the landing zone to make it safer for the troops as they landed. The noise was extremely loud and dense, and the ground shook with each explosion. The concussion from the blasts made every tree and branch shiver, as did we. My heart was pounding as we took cover in the woodline, diving behind trees and shrubs, waiting for orders. All too soon we were ordered to start walking toward our NDP (night defensive perimeter), where we would dig in for the night. After a distance of only six hundred meters, the three infantry companies formed a perimeter in the middle of a clearing, and began to dig. It was nearly four o'clock in the afternoon. The Big Red One procedure for establishing a night defensive perimeter was arduous. All of the holes were positioned carefully to maintain complete security around the perimeter; dirt from the holes was used to fill sandbags for walls around the hole, the sleeping area in the rear of the hole, and the roof overhead. Firing lanes were then drawn up for each hole, crisscrossing to ensure that not one square inch of territory to the front was uncovered. After the hole was dug, metal bars were placed on top, and piled over with more sandbags. The hole was both a killing apparatus and security fortress; two portals stuck out from the front, from which we would fire into the oncoming enemy, and the portals were the only exposed section of the hole to enemy fire and mortar.

Since we did not arrive at our NDP until four o'clock, darkness fell before we had even completed digging, and the monsoon rain began pouring down on us, making this night one of my most miserable nights in Vietnam, a story covered earlier. We did not finish fortifying the holes until after one o'clock in the morning, at which time we began guard duty, and were allowed to catch a couple hours sleep. Diehl, Fierro, Adams, and I were in one hole; the M-60 machine gun bunker was to our left, and Pritch's hole, which included Freppon, Ciliberti, and Haymon, was next to the machine gunner.

The battalion was now prepared for battle, with Bravo, Charlie, and Delta Companies at the ready. Alpha Company was in the rear for a two-week rest. Our battalion commander, Colonel Cavazos, had established his headquarters in the center of the three-hundred-man perimeter. The jungle to our front was dense, so the foxholes seemed like they were stacked on top of each other, which gave us comfort, knowing that the firing lanes would be concentrated and precise. We were in the thick of the "boonies," with nothing but trees and bushes to our immediate front. If the enemy had attacked on our first night, with the rain pouring down, we would have been at a huge disadvantage, with no cover, no light, and in a disorganized formation. Fortunately, the Viet Cong, or "Victor Charlie" as we called him, had decided not to make his presence known that first night. This resulted in our ability to dig our night defenses, and rest for what we knew was going to be our first taste of combat.

The following day we patrolled some of the thickest jungle imaginable, in hot, humid weather, but no enemy was found. My squad had ambush patrol the second night in the field, but turned out to be uneventful as well. Returning to the perimeter the next morning, we spent the day improving our positions, cleaning our weapons, and talking. We knew that if we didn't find the enemy soon, we would be ordered to break camp, be flown to another area, and have to dig in all over again. Such was the life of a combat soldier in the First Infantry Division. Rumors fill the air when in the field, which was one way of responding to fears and questions about what was to come.

It was late in the afternoon on October 6. We had just finished our delicious hot meal, flown in from Di An, and were sitting around our holes just shooting the bull. A rain storm was approaching from the west, and we could tell darkness would come early. I was lying down behind the hole, with my feet propped up on the wall of sandbags, which surrounded the two-man sleeping area. Diehl, Fierro, Adams, and I were discussing who would go first on guard duty, and we all were looking forward to another quiet night, and a few hours sleep. Suddenly, the silence was sliced with the sounds of explosions all around us. The ground shook with a loud, hollow pounding sound, like THUD, THUD, THUD. I was terrified at first, for we were all caught off guard. I jumped up to see what was happening, and saw everyone running in all directions, heading for the foxholes. It was mass confusion for just a few seconds, and I could hear screams from the officers and NCOs weaved among the sounds of explosions—"In the holes—incoming!" The Viet Cong were indiscriminately hitting our perimeter with mortars, and they were exploding throughout the open area around the foxholes. Soldiers were diving into the holes, others grabbed their helmets and rifles and ran as fast as they could for cover. Within a split second I threw my helmet on my head, grabbed my M-16, an ammunition belt, and jumped into the hole with Diehl and Fierro. Adams, our squad leader, sat on the steps that led into the hole, peering over the roof of sandbags to the front. I loaded my rifle, and placed it in the porthole, and got ready to fire. It then began to rain mercilessly, a perfect cover for a Viet Cong ground attack. It seemed that the enemy's timing was extremely well coordinated with the monsoon weather. It grew dark, and the mortar barrage lasted for about an hour, but gradually died down. The four of us were packed tightly in the hole, and the even the Delta Company first sergeant, Sergeant King, "Top King," we called him, came over and sat behind Adams. The rain was so hard that it began pouring down inside the hole, dripping through the sandbags, and before I knew it, I was knee deep in water and mud, to the point where I had to jerk my foot to loosen my boots from the thick mud.

As the mortars ceased falling from the sky, Colonel Cavazos ordered aerial flares to be launched all around the perimeter, which illuminated the clearing around the outside of the perimeter, about fifty meters in front of the holes, beyond which lay the thick jungle. This was the "fire zone," and anyone caught there would be deemed enemy. There were so many flares that it almost seemed like day, and that's when the fighting started, first on the other side of the perimeter, then gradually moving to Delta Company's side. Top King yelled down into our hole to start firing. At what, I had no idea, because the rain was so dense that I could hardly see more than ten meters to my front. I opened up with my M-16, firing two and three round bursts, as we were taught in training. The sky lit up with tracer bullets flying and ricocheting in all directions, bouncing off trees, sandbags, the ground—everywhere. As I was firing, I thought to myself that this was my first taste of combat. I looked at my watch, and it was almost 8:00 p.m. I quickly thought of Sally back home, and what she would be doing at this moment—probably starting one of her classes, back with all my friends. This comforting thought lasted just a split second, because the noise and shouting brought me back to reality, but it was a moment I will never forget, and I felt strangely close to Sally even though we were worlds apart.

The firing continued, but we were told to cut back in order to conserve ammunition. The rain was so hard I still could not see any enemy soldiers to my front, in the small fire zone framed by my porthole. The aerial flares continued, lighting the sky and the ground to the front, and as they approached the ground, shadows became bigger, and danced side to side from the flares blowing in the wind in their descent. Suddenly, bullets ripped into the sandbags on the side of my porthole, and Diehl's as well, and slammed into the wall inside the foxhole. We crouched down, realizing that we were inches away from being shot in the head. We shot back, in anger that the enemy had come so close to killing us, even though we still could not see them. I was firing into the woodline just fifty meters to my front, thinking they had to be there, hiding behind trees and in trenches. My M-16 then jammed, and I let Fierro take my place at the porthole as I unlocked the stock and tried to clear out the mud causing the jam. "Damn rifle," I said, but got it back to working condition in just a few minutes.

I remember my feelings well in my first combat experience. The Viet Cong apparently had tried to assault our position in the perimeter, but were pushed back. When firing for the first time, I was nervous and fearful, knowing that the flash of my rifle would expose my position, and could easily be targeted, which indeed happened when bullets came flying through our portholes, just missing our heads All through basic and advanced infantry training, I fired at pop-up targets; now they were men, and these men were firing back, desperately trying to kill me. I wondered if any of my bullets were hitting the enemy in the tree line. I was cold and wet, and began to shiver in the deepening water, but I am sure my nervousness added a little rhythm to my already shaking body.

The fighting stopped on Delta Company's side of the perimeter at midnight. So did the rain. We began guard duty, and took shifts to try and catch some sleep. The remainder of the night was quiet, but eerie. A fog settled in all around us, and the aerial flares kept up all night long, the light from which produced a milky, orange appearance to the sky. Everything was drenched and muddy. I slept only from 4:00 to 5:00 a.m., so with the ambush patrol the night before, I had only managed one hour sleep in the last forty eight. I soon discovered the irregularity and unpredictability of life in the field in combat.

As the sun rose in the east the next morning, our clothes and backpacks began to dry out. In a surprise visit, Major General Hay, the First Infantry Division commander, came out to the field to talk with the men of Delta Company. He made his rounds from hole to hole, with small talk of how we felt, did we have enough ammunition and so on. I thought it was a terrible risk for him to take, with the enemy position only fifty meters to the front, but it felt strangely comforting to see a general walking among his troops, encouraging and congratulating us in our first battle.

The First Infantry Division reported our first battle, in the division's magazine *Danger Forward*, which said,

> At 1500 hours on 6 October the "Swamp Rats" received five 60mm mortar rounds in their NDP. The perimeter consisted of B Company in the north, C Company in the east, and D Company in the west. The NDP was in a natural clearing with the trip flares that the 1st Battalion, 18th Infantry had planted among the trees. Claymores either in the trees or in the clearing near the treeline were detonated by the Big Red One infantrymen from their bunkers. Many of the mines were

replaced by men who crawled outside the perimeter during lulls in the fighting. At 2317 hours a barrage of 60 to 70 82mm mortar rounds rained upon the NDP, followed immediately by a ground attack on D Company from the south. This final attack was the heaviest, and for the first time, the Viet Cong could be seen moving out of the treeline. At times the enemy soldiers were able to advance within 10 meters of the "Dogface" bunkers, but a heavy volume of fire and close-in artillery support forced them to retreat and break contact at 2345 hours. A sweep the following morning turned up 24 enemy bodies and numerous documents.

From that day on, the Operation Shenandoah (the name given to our battle, as we learned), daytime patrols would advance just two or three hundred meters from the perimeter before we would be ambushed by an entrenched enemy. Colonel Cavazos was a conservative war tactician; as he told us when we first met him in Di An in July. As soon as our patrols were ambushed, he ordered our retreat back to the perimeter, and immediately called in air strikes and artillery on our positions as we withdrew. On one such patrol, Delta Company was on point, leading the two-company patrol through the dense jungle several hundred meters from our NDP. On the patrol, we walked right into a Viet Cong ambush; when the bullets started flying and hitting all around us, we all fell on the ground instantly. It was an extremely helpless and terrifying experience, as bullets came at us from all directions, from up in the trees, from behind bushes and tree stumps. We fired back in the direction from which the bullets came, although we still could not see our enemy. I fired two or three round bursts, then rolled three feet to my left or right, and fired again. We had been taught to keep moving if there was no cover. It was in this battle that I first had the sensation that an enemy soldier had me framed in his rifle sight. It is a fear I carry with me to this day. Fortunately, as with the previous patrols, we were told to pull back to the perimeter, and allow the air strikes and artillery to finish the fighting for us. In our withdrawal, we had to run through a hail of bullets streaming down from above. I saw them hit all around me as they ripped through the leaves and brush beside me, and at this we picked up the pace of our retreat. I felt helpless and very scared—I was sure I was going to be hit. For a moment, I lost sight of Pritch, whom I was following in line through the jungle. I panicked for just an instant, thinking I was lost. I quickly found him, and saw his gritting teeth, and his blackened face filled with terror and fear. We finally made it back to the perimeter, and lost three men from our platoon, although none was killed. Haymon was the most seriously wounded, and was airlifted back to the hospital at Di An. Each day that followed repeated the same routine—patrol, ambush, followed by artillery and air strikes. For some reason, the Viet Cong, however, did not attack our perimeter again while we were on Operation Shenandoah.

My most unforgettable moment of this battle, one in which I actually felt the face of death breathing down my neck, occurred a few nights later. Ambush patrols were sent out each night, a squad-sized force which sets up several hundred meters from the perimeter at dusk, and waits for the enemy to arrive. On most nights this exercise is nothing more than a tense calm, and no sleep from the group of ten or twelve soldiers. If the enemy wanders near the ambush, the squad leader decides whether to fight, or let them pass, a decision based on the size of the enemy force.

The Big Red One always had a platoon-sized force of men accompany the ambush patrol to their site about an hour before dusk, then return to the perimeter. The average platoon contained about forty men at full strength (which was never). My platoon had the assignment to accompany an ambush squad one night, and my squad was on point. Steve Diehl was point man, and I was second, followed by Pritch, Fierro, and Ciliberti. When we reached the ambush site, the five of us were ordered to perform a "cloverleaf" maneuver. Cloverleaf was a tactical term for a rifle squad making a reconnaissance sweep through an unsecured area to determine if any enemy soldiers were present. The five of us were ordered to approach a woodline about fifty meters to our right, to determine if the enemy was hiding there. Some considered this a suicide mission, but the safety of fifty other men depended upon ensuring the security of the ambush site. As we moved out toward the woodline, it started to grow dark, and I had an eerie premonition that Viet Cong machine guns and rifles were aiming at us from behind the darkness of the jungle ahead, and at any moment they would open up, killing us instantly. Thought of a rifle sight trained on my head again popped into my mind, and I was *sure* I saw a face in the darkness of the trees ahead. Suddenly, a bush about ten meters to our front shook violently, and the safeties on all five of our rifles clicked simultaneously as we jerked up the barrels of the rifles in its direction. A bird then flew out of the bush, and Diehl turned to me, with a look on his face I will never forget—white with fear and cold with sweat. I looked at Pritch, and he appeared as shaken as Diehl and me. There was no smile on their faces now, like back at Di An, but a somber, strained expression of fear, one which made us all feel and appear much older. Calming down, we again put our rifles on safety, and approached the woodline, which was unoccupied, then walked back to the platoon, said goodbye to the ambush patrol, and returned to the NDP.

When one experiences something new and unique in their life, it leaves an unforgettable, vivid impression in the mind. The feelings I experienced in those brief, terrifying moments have stayed with me to this day. The five of us were totally exposed in an open field, and as we approached the woodline, I searched every tree limb and twig for movement, a blunt projection like a rifle, or for a face. In my fear, a tree stump apparently looked like the face of a Viet Cong soldier, and I knew that my imagination and nerves were being stretched to the limit. I actually thought that I may die in that open field, and felt a rifle sight pointed at my head. My heart was pounding so loud that I could hear it, for the only other sounds at that moment were our footsteps in the grass, and the silence added to my fear. My buddies felt the same, and in that moment we were united not only by fear, but by the same fate of whatever awaited us. I actually saw in my mind the angry stare of a Viet Cong soldier.

Fortunately, my feelings of being watched were wrong, but I do believe they made us more alert and prepared. If there were Viet Cong soldiers in that jungle, they let us pass, since the five of us represented a smaller prize than a platoon or company of Big Red One soldiers. I remember briefly thinking of Sally, and my family, during those tense moments, and how they would react to the news of my being killed in combat. The five of us rejoined our platoon, and returned to the perimeter of foxholes, and as we slumped down around the hole, we melted with relief. We discussed how we "dodged a bullet," and talked about the bird that almost gave us heart attacks. Fear eventually turned to laughs, but I know that experience aged me considerably.

Operation Shenandoah was the first combat mission for the new Delta Company of the 1/18th Regiment of the First Infantry Division. Throughout the twelve days of the campaign, Delta Company lost fewer men than Bravo or Charlie Companies.

Lt. Col. Richard Cavazos, second from the left, with fellow battalion commanders on Operation Shenandoah, October 1967.
[PHOTO FROM *DANGER FORWARD*. PHOTOGRAPHER, SSG GERARD FORKEN]

Maybe it was luck; two Bravo Company ambushes were triggered when the Viet Cong wandered into the ambush area at night, and both companies suffered more casualties than Delta in our unsuccessful patrol probes around the perimeter. One night, a Bravo Company ambush patrol had to return to the NDP in the middle of the night, suffering two dead and nine wounded. The body of one of the two KIAs (killed in action) was left out in the darkness, and when a Bravo Company patrol found it in the morning, the body was stripped of all clothing. Delta Company had not one KIA, although we had several wounded. Our success instilled immense pride in the soldiers of the new Delta Company.

Ambushes serve an integral part of First Infantry Division battle tactics. With a battalion-sized force of men (around three hundred), each of the three rifle companies would station a squad on ambush in front of its sector of the perimeter, a few hundred meters out in the jungle. The ambush would be the first line of defense to any enemy movement, or if triggered, to kill a manageable force of enemy soldiers. The ambush patrol moves out just before dusk, and sets up in a small triangle, with three of four men on each side, near a path, road, or area where enemy movement might occur. I viewed these tactics as the most dangerous we performed in Vietnam. Claymore mines are set up in front of all three sides of the ambush. Claymores are electronically detonated mines which can be triggered by pushing a button. They are spread around the ambush site, and are detonated when the enemy walks into its path. Absolute silence is understood by all on an ambush; the main objective is to catch the enemy as they approach the NDP, or take intelligence as an enemy patrol passes by. The key elements to a successful ambush are silence and surprise, and if strict silence is not followed, the ambush patrol's safety can be compromised. I had never been on an ambush which was triggered, luckily experiencing just a loss of one night's sleep, and the intense anxiety of being "out there" in the darkness with just a squad of men. There were nights, however, when we heard voices, and saw lights several meters to our front, as the Viet Cong passed by, unaware we were there ready to fight. Our reward for coming in the next day was staying in our holes, relaxing, while the remainder of the company participated in the usual search and destroy missions.

During the two weeks on Operation Shenandoah, the relationship with my buddies changed dramatically. We grew up quickly in combat. Not only were we closer together as friends, and tighter as a fighting unit, but we saw expressions on each other's faces that were new to us. Keep in mind that most of us had been together since basic training, so we had been friends for almost ten months. The infantryman in Vietnam usually arrived in country as a replacement, joining an infantry company without knowing a soul. We were tight, and now we were combat veterans. Up until Shenandoah, our work together was routine and rather boring, but in combat, we had placed our lives in danger for the first time, tasted the fear of battle, and came away more mature and appreciative for the friends we had. Gone were the peaceful days of sitting around the cots at Di An, drinking beer, and talking or singing our favorite songs. Smiles and carefree faces were replaced with fear and strain. We grew more serious in the attitude about our work together, and our presence in Vietnam. I know that any one of us would have sacrificed his life for another. I wondered what was happening to all of us, most of whom were just nineteen or twenty years of age. We had suddenly grown up, maturing in our thoughts and actions, and cared for each other much more deeply. Combat was responsible for all of this.

Back home as civilians we had experienced no life threatening situation and no degree of discomfort and sacrifice we now felt. But we were not civilians now, we were soldiers, fighting an unpopular war in a distant land. Our distance from home was made harsher because mail took five days, and often when Sally received my letters, my entire situation had then changed. And even then, there were no live video reports; news networks made reports with cameras on film, which also took days to reach the viewers back home, due to lack of satellite transmission in 1967. The Vietnam War might as well have been fought on the moon.

Jack Freppon and I were once college students at the University of Cincinnati, Fierro had a wife back in New Mexico, Pritch was a playboy surfer kid in California, but now we were all soldiers, with the same rank and privilege, and though our skin color and ethnicity may have differed, we were brothers then, and remain brothers now. The only family you have in Vietnam is your squad, and each soldier has a job to do, with only one goal in mind—to stay alive and kill the enemy.

In Vietnam I came to loathe the Viet Cong. We saw their atrocities, and our hatred for our enemy grew every day we fought him in battle. Paradoxically, we held them in high respect, because they were a formidable foe. They were guerrilla fighters, and even though they held the home ground, they knew the geography well, which played to their advantage, and were accustomed to the brutal climate, they were agile, elusive, brave, and determined. They were also stubborn and fierce, traits we saw close up on Operation Shenandoah. We faced an enemy well equipped with the latest Chinese and Russian weaponry; the Chinese AK-47 automatic rifle was less accurate than our M-16s, but endured the tropical climate much better than our rifles, and experienced fewer episodes of jamming. The unit we were up against on this operation, the 271st Viet Cong Regiment, was well supplied with RPGs (rocket propelled grenades), a most effective weapon used in blowing up bunkers and sandbag-lined foxholes.

The main advantage American troops had in Vietnam was the helicopter, allowing quick assaults in war zones within hours. Our infantry tactics were reinforced with precision air strikes and artillery barrages, both used to perfection by Colonel Cavazos on Shenandoah.

Our enemy had unique advantages as well, and he used them very effectively. The Vietnam War was, mostly, a guerrilla war, where the U.S. troops owned the daytime, and Charlie ruled the night. The Viet Cong, North Vietnamese, and the Viet Minh before them, had been fighting this war against the Western powers since the end of World War II. The North Vietnamese, and their allies in the South, were determined, brave, and inexhaustible. They were committed to the fighting until victory or their defeat was decided, while the U.S. troops were made up of soldiers who were desperately fighting to stay alive for 365 days. The burden on us was to do our best, keep ourselves and our buddies safe, fighting not only the enemy, but the intense heat and humidity of the jungle, flooding monsoon rains, endless days of patrolling, endless nights of ambushes and lack of sleep.

Looking back at my tour in Vietnam, with more than forty years of wisdom and history to color my perspective of those days, I often remember the innocence which guided me as a dedicated and determined soldier. I was filled with anger that, at least at the time when I served, the war had yet to absorb the national consciousness, and especially with respect to my friends at home, they really did not seem to care. I felt that the comfort and freedom Americans enjoyed at home kept them removed from the few who served. What was a distant, irrelevant "military action" to civilians at home was a daily life and death struggle for thousands of young men and women, in that terrible war. I remember discussing with my buddies how this seeming indifference was extremely disheartening to us; how if those at home were faced with losing a friend, fighting an unseen enemy, living days and nights in fear and exhaustion, maybe they would better understand the sacrifices our military was making in Vietnam, and more visibly support our efforts. I tried to imagine my friends back home in my college fraternity, and how they would feel if they suddenly found themselves on patrol or ambush, in a firefight and digging foxholes until one o'clock in the morning. I imagined some of my friends getting wounded and dying, and asked how would they feel then? My new friends in Vietnam were not just soldiers, men on whom I depended, and for whom I risked my life to ensure their safety, but were "citizen soldiers," who had jobs, girlfriends, families, and eighteen or nineteen years of growing up before they found themselves in this distant war. I was proud to be a soldier in

Delta Company, proud to wear a uniform, and proud to be best friends with a brave group of soldiers who faced the hardships of combat, and felt the sweetness of a brotherhood forged in battle.

Our squad was my new family, and we cared and watched out for each other every minute of the day. I grew closer to these men in a shorter span than I did with any other person in my life, except for my future wife, Sally. These feelings still hold true forty-five years later. Combat and mutual sacrifice have permanently altered the filter with which I call someone a friend. By that, I mean the degree of friendship I feel; no other experience could possible bring me closer to a group of men than what we all saw in Vietnam. Some of my friends did not make it home. Those that did, I still call brothers, and enjoy the privilege of growing old with them and their families. Lt. Mel Brav, one of the second lieutenants in Delta Company, said years later at one of our reunions, that "we had the rose-colored glasses" removed at an early age, having to grow up quickly, facing death and losing friends, all of which would take its toll in the years following the war.

It was a short two weeks on Operation Shenandoah, and on October 15 we were airlifted out of the war zone to Song Be, a small village about twenty miles south of the Cambodian border, a relatively secure area. Just like Quon Loi, our days were filled with exhausting patrols during the day, ambushes at night, but at least quiet and routine duty, which was welcomed by all of us.

The relative quiet did not relieve us of the arduous task of building a new NDP, complete with Big Red One fortified foxholes. Ten days later, however, on October 25, we flew to Lai Khe, about fifty miles due south, a First Infantry Division base camp, for some well deserved rest. We were to be housed in tents with cots, and looked forward to hot meals and showers. However, upon our arrival, the tents were not available, so we were asked to set up our sleeping bags and ponchos in an open area, until more permanent sleeping arrangements were made. I didn't argue; the ground was hard, but the quiet, and no guard duty, allowed for a good night's sleep ahead. We all went to the club that night and drank too many beers, told war stories, and listened to a Vietnamese band attempt to play the current hits of the 1960s. I ate what I thought was a hamburger, my first since coming to Vietnam. I learned later to never do that again. As one of my friends told me, today's pet dog is tomorrow's beef patty. Nevertheless, I went to sleep that night looking forward to some relaxation, good food, letters from home, and most of all, sleep.

    All too suddenly, George Adams and Steve Pritchett were leaning over me at four thirty in the morning, telling me to get up and pack my things. Both of them were walking around, stumbling over grumbling soldiers, trying to wake up the entire company. I remember my heart sinking, as I packed my gear and assembled my weapons. We were moving to a helicopter pad as soon as daylight broke. Fresh ammunition was passed out to all of us, and I packed about twenty magazines of bullets in my back pack, along with a couple days of C rations. Rumors immediately filled the air where we were going, probably all of them false, but one thing was certain, we were headed back into combat. When we were in the air, the NCOs told us we were heading into a hot LZ near Loc Ninh, a small village on the border of Cambodia, which had been overrun the night before by the Viet Cong and North Vietnamese. Three First Infantry Division battalions were being airlifted to Loc Ninh, and would be positioned between the village and the Cambodian border, to serve as a blocking force against the enemy as he tried to retreat to the safe sanctuary jungle of Cambodia.

We were about to face a hard core enemy force, made up of the 271st Viet Cong Regiment and the 165th North Vietnamese Army (NVA). It was late October, and enemy attacks along the Cambodian border were picking up. The approaching battle of Loc Ninh was a prelude to a tremendous troop buildup by the enemy, as he prepared to launch the Tet Offensive of January 1968. As we neared the LZ, we knew nothing about our enemy, did not know the significance of what was about to happen. We clutched our rifles, checked our ammo, and hardly spoke. The noise of the rotor blades made it too hard to communicate anyway.

The landscape below was beautiful. Loc Ninh is situated in a part of the country dominated by rubber tree plantations, like in Quon Loi. Miles and miles of trees lined with perfect precision, with a three foot trench between every other row for irrigation in the raining season. Landing on the ground was uneventful, and we immediately headed toward our designated NDP. Bravo Company remained at Di An for this mission, so our battalion force at Loc Ninh was Alpha, Charlie, and Delta Companies.

It was midafternoon on October 27, and we began digging our holes among the rows of rubber trees. Thankfully, the dense foliage of the trees, about twenty feet high, shaded the hot afternoon sun. Yet, unlike Shenandoah, our enemy did not give us the luxury of digging in before he made his presence known.

As soon as we started digging, snipers, just one hundred meters to our front, opened up on our side of the perimeter, making us dive for cover behind trees and in the trenches. Colonel Cavazos immediately ordered Charlie Company to saddle up and head in the direction of the fire. As the men approached an area just down a few rows of trees, they were ambushed at close range, and a firefight ensued. We felt helpless, as we sat there and listened to the firing, just out of our sight over a hill. Everyone was anxious to help Charlie Company, and Colonel Cavazos evidently agreed, because the order came to move out in the same direction to provide assistance for Charlie Company. We hadn't walked more than fifty meters when we met Charlie Company's retreat back to the perimeter. The only fighting that occurred for us that day was providing cover as the men of Charlie Company walked in two rows back to the NDP. The most shocking, sobering sight was watching soldiers carrying back the bodies of their dead buddies from the ambush. Four men carried each body, one holding onto each limb; the deceased soldiers' heads were limp, and swung back and forth with each step, with towels dripping wet with blood placed respectfully over their heads. I thought of how these men were alive just minutes ago, but now their lives were over, much too quickly. I thought of their parents and loved ones, who had no idea this had happened, and would not find out for days. I did not know these men, but the sight of their lifeless, limp bodies brought a lump to my throat. I still had not grown used to death,

A typical rubber tree plantation.
Note the precisely placed rows of trees for miles.

I didn't think I ever would. These men had plans of returning home, as did we all, but fate, and God, knew differently. I wondered to myself, on this hot afternoon, where was their soul? I did not have the luxury of more introspection, for the order came to return to the NDP and to dig in.

For the next six hours, our digging was accompanied by a constant barrage of artillery shells exploding all around the perimeter. Darkness had come, and aerial flares were launched in all directions, but they didn't help. Even though the trunks of the rubber trees were bare of branches except near the top, about twenty feet in the air, their dense foliage prevented much light from the flares reaching the ground. We worked throughout the night, and took turns on guard duty, allowing about one hour of sleep for everyone in the battalion.

The next day on patrol we picked up various weapons which the enemy had thrown away in their flight from the artillery barrage. I was not prepared for the sight of the enemy bodies decimated by the artillery. Mounds of nothing but body parts were left in piles, which we could smell as we approached them. It was impossible to make a body count from the remains, but we could tell the toll was in the dozens. Their uniforms confirmed the enemy we faced—a hardcore regiment of Viet Cong, and the NVA. Their uniforms were brown, others green, complete with pith helmets.

The next day was more memorable. By now I had lost count of the calendar, as my letters to Sally from Loc Ninh attest— some were written with a question mark in the upper right hand corner where I usually placed the date. *Danger Forward* quotes,

> The following morning, Alpha Company of the 1/18th Infantry made contact with an estimated battalion of the 165th North Vietnamese Regiment south of the "Dogface" NDP. The enemy battalion was occupying trench-

lines atop a sloping piece of terrain called Hill 203. The trenches were elongated drainage ditches between rows of rubber trees. As soon as the firing erupted, it was heard at the NDP. Colonel Cavazos immediately organized Delta Company and the CDIG company (Special Forces) to reinforce Alpha Company. Within minutes these reinforcements, together with the battalion command group (Cavazos), were moving toward the contact. As Delta Company approached within 200 meters of Alpha Company, it made contact with the enemy unit that was attempting to envelop the latter.

Colonel Cavazos had ordered Alpha Company to move out on a patrol midmorning, toward a designation named "Hill 203." As with Charlie Company, firing was heard when they reached three hundred meters from the perimeter, but this time, the ambush was on the opposite side of our NDP, suggesting to us that the enemy had us surrounded. We stood by our foxholes, weapons locked and loaded, listening helplessly, as the fighting continued. Again, Cavazos ordered Delta Company into formation, and we began our march toward the fighting. We moved in a column of twos through the rubber trees, down a soft slope to the base of a hill. The hill was on our left, and the trees and trenches were positioned left to right, parallel to our column. Suddenly, a hail of bullets rippled all around us on our left, from trenches up on the hill. We dove for cover in the trenches, and Colonel Cavazos, who was walking with the men of Delta Company, ordered us to return fire up on the hill. For fifteen minutes the entire forest was filled with ear-shattering small arms fire, and bullets, lit with tracers, ricocheting in every direction from the trees. Cavazos began positioning Alpha and Delta Company into one line at the base of the hill, telling us to stay low, but return fire "at will." Having the colonel right there with us was a comfort. Most battalion commanders led their troops from a safer harbor—either from a helicopter above, out of range of fire, or from the HQ position back at the NDP, staying in contact with his company commanders by radio. Cavazos had nothing to do with that. His call sign was "Dogface 6," and he wanted to be with his boys on the front line. That's why we respected him so much. On this day, our battalion commander was in the trenches, shouting orders, cursing and prodding his lieutenants and captains, but most importantly, he was *leading* his troops on the ground.

We were now in one line at the base of the hill. Delta Company in the middle, Alpha Company to our right, and to our left, a small band of South Vietnamese special forces, led by a U.S. Army Green Beret captain. The South Vietnamese were a band of nonuniformed montagnards, volunteers who lived in the mountains, and hated the Viet Cong. They were young, mostly boys in their late teens or early twenties, and were equipped with carbines and pistols. There were about 250 of us lined up at the bottom of Hill 203, in a trench, looking up to where the fighting was about to take place. Cavazos ordered air strikes and artillery to rain down on the enemy bunkers on the hill; he started the bombardment at the top, and called in the strikes downward, in succession, which helped to block the enemy's retreat. It was a mastery of battlefield tactics, and we sat there in awe as the explosions came nearer to us, like steps of a monster getting closer. When the blasts approached about fifty meters out, we could feel the heat of the napalm, and had to duck as pieces of shrapnel, wood, and dirt fell all around us from the blasts. I had never been so close to one of our artillery barrages. Through the smoke and fire, we could see enemy soldiers running around on the hill, from trench to trench, for protection. We were ordered to hold our fire until the barrage, which lasted for a good hour, was completed.

A deafening silence ensued following the bombardment, and Cavazos gave the order to move out. We stepped out of the trenches and began moving up the hill, slowly at first, as the NCOs were yelling at us to "stay on line," and to watch out for bunkers and snipers. I cannot remember who was on my right or left at first, my full attention was straight ahead. Alpha Company, on our right, was hit almost immediately as we started our advance, and shortly, weapons opened up in front of us. We were fortunate that the trenches provided excellent cover, and we once again dove into them, as we began our assault. Enemy machine guns were ripping up the dirt right in front of my face, and explosions were hitting our trenches, and the trees in front and behind us. The blasts were coming from RPGs, and there was a frightful number of them exploding all around us. As soon as we hit the dirt the NCOs started yelling for us to keep moving, cursing at us, telling us to move from tree to tree, trench to trench. I was crawling on my belly, with bullets zipping overhead, ricocheting off the trees, hitting the ground behind us. The tracers were everywhere—ours were red, the VC and North Vietnamese used green and white. The forest was lit up with them, zinging in all directions. I could also hear the *woosh* of the RPGs that zoomed over our heads before blasting a tree. After a few minutes of this very slow advance up the hill, I came to a VC bunker just a few meters directly to my front. There were four of them, and they were raining down automatic weapons fire at me, and the men to my left and right. George Adams, my squad leader, was next to me, and he told me to keep firing on automatic, as he and I gave cover fire for Ron Campsey, and our platoon medic, Frank Passantino, to advance on the bunker from the left. As they approached the trench, they fired their weapons and killed all four enemy soldiers. At that instant an RPG blast hit the tree above them, and Campsey fell to the ground with a wound in his leg. Steve Diehl, on my right, immediately jumped up and yelled for Campsey, and began running toward the bunker. I remember him yelling "Campsey, Campsey . . . you all right?" He and Diehl were best friends, having trained together since basic. He found Campsey, who amazingly only had a minor wound in his leg from the blast.

Having eliminated the first bunker, we again came across another, just about twenty or thirty meters up the hill. Adams and I were told to advance, and try to eliminate the bunker with grenades. We both crawled toward the bunker, keeping our heads down, trying to use the terrain as cover, and when we thought we were close enough, Adams told me to "empty my magazine," meaning a full automatic blast of twenty rounds, as he attempted to toss two grenades into the bunker. We were still too far for him to reach the bunker with the grenades, and now, our position was compromised. The noise of the battle was so loud I could hardly hear Adams, although we were right next to each other. I saw Shelby Davidson and Jack Freppon crawling up on our left flank toward the bunker, trying to find access for a grenade toss. Adams and I again provided cover for them, and both threw a couple of grenades directly into the trench. Freppon and Davidson were still on their bellies after the blasts, and at that moment one of the South Vietnamese montagnards ran up to the trench, with nothing more than a 45-caliber pistol, and emptied his clip into the trench. He reached down, pulled up an AK-47 automatic rifle from one of the dead soldiers, and fired in the trench until the clip was empty. He then held the rifle in the air, waving it as a trophy. I believe the grenades had killed the enemy soldiers, but this brave act by one of our young allied soldiers inspired us all that day. As he waved the rifle in the air, I looked around to see who I was near. Everyone was yelling, cheering, and raising their fists and M-16s in the air as well. Davidson turned around, saw Adams and me, and almost cried with enthusiasm. His fist was raised in the air, his teeth were gritting through his blackened, sweaty, smiling face. It was strange seeing these smiling, shouting soldiers in the middle of battle. Men were dying, but we were exuberant with joy, and found renewed courage. Cavazos knew we had an opportunity as well, and ordered the troops to pick up the pace of our advance. We apparently eliminated the front line of the enemy's defense, because our advance became easier. We ran up the hill when we could, jumping from trench to trench, firing as we moved. My heart was pounding with exhaustion and fear, but the adrenaline drove me up that hill. We fought from tree to tree, and began seeing the toll of our firepower as we advanced. I leapt over trenches filled with enemy dead. One of our machine gunners stopped at one trench, and kept firing rounds into the already dead bodies. I remember stopping, turning around, and yelling at him "That's enough . . . how many times can you kill a soldier?"

Halfway up the hill we were ordered to stop, and allow Alpha Company and the montagnards to catch up and get on line. This was the first time I took stock of my situation. My clothes were soaked with sweat, sap, and blood. The sticky white sap from the wounded rubber trees was everywhere, on the ground, on us and on our weapons. We rested for only five minutes, and were ordered to move out once again. Toward the summit the assault involved less fighting. But the forest was littered with fallen trees, which were blackened and decimated, and dead Viet Cong bodies were everywhere. Most of this collateral damage occurred from the air strikes, and the filthy stink of napalm made me sick.

As we reached the summit of Hill 203, some of us sat down,

some just fell on the ground, totally spent. Frank Fierro and Steve Pritchett were next to me, and both lit up a cigarette, puffing the nervousness out of their bodies. There were no smiles this time; we were shaking from exhaustion, and spoke very little. The assault had lasted one hour, but seemed like the entire day. A man named Best, from the first squad, was lying on the ground with a bandage wrapped around his head, and blood dripping down his face. My M-16 rifle was so hot from firing it, that I had to lean it against a tree. I could not touch the barrel, which was still smoking. I had used up eleven of my sixteen magazines, meaning I had fired over two hundred rounds of ammunition in the assault. Some were completely out of ammo. For the first time that day, I starting thinking of home, and Sally sleeping comfortably in her bed in the dorm. It was midafternoon, and in Cincinnati it would be the middle of the night before. She seemed safe and protected to me, and I said to myself that I was helping to keep her safe by being here in Vietnam.

After a few minutes of rest and introspection, Colonel Cavazos ordered us to return to the perimeter, because darkness was approaching. He also ordered us to gather all of the enemy weapons, any documents which could be found on the dead, and make a body count on the way down the hill. On our descent I saw the bodies of the American dead, as they were being carried down the hill on stretchers, wrapped in rubber body bags. There was a clearing in the forest at the base of the hill, and several Red Cross helicopters had landed to take the bodies back to Di An. We stopped for a moment as the bodies were placed on the choppers, and I noticed some of the men who were their buddies were crying. As with the first day of fighting at Loc Ninh, seeing these dead American soldiers shocked me; even though I was surrounded by many of enemy dead, I still was saddened at the sight of these body bags, and tried to make sense of it all. Unbelievably, not one soldier in Delta Company was killed this day, although a dozen or so were wounded. Alpha Company lost six men in the assault. Our count of the enemy dead on the way down the hill totaled eighty-three, although we were sure many more bodies were dragged away before the fighting began.

Colonel Cavazos later was awarded the Distinguished Service Cross for his leadership in the assault in Hill 203. Following is an excerpt from his DSC commendation:

> When the fighting reached such close quarters that supporting fire could no longer be used, he completely disregarded his own safety and personally led a determined assault on the enemy positions. The assault was carried out with such force and aggressiveness that the Viet Cong were overrun and fled their trenches. Colonel Cavazos then directed artillery fire on the hilltop, and the insurgents were destroyed as they ran. His brilliant leadership in the face of grave danger resulted in maximum enemy casualties and the capture of many hostile weapons.

Delta Company distinguished itself in this battle. *Danger Forward* reported,

> As the Big Red One soldiers moved up the hill, an enemy machine gunner in a bunker opened fire. Specialist 4 Ronald Campsey, PFC Jack Freppon and PFC Joseph Hayman [Pete Haymon] spotted the emplacement, and with their comrades providing covering fire, began to maneuver against it. Nearing the complex, they were taken under fire by the enemy, but succeeded in overrunning it, and killing the three North Vietnamese inside, thus enabling the remainder of the company

to advance. Seven enemy trenches were overrun, putting the NVA soldiers in full flight to the southwest through a draw.

As I walked back to the perimeter, I carried with me several ammunition pouches which I removed from the dead, and several RPG rockets. The RPG was an abundant weapon used by the enemy, and was most effective in close in fighting. Shaped like a bazooka, the rocket was placed in the front of the tube, and fired from the shoulder. Its aim was precise, and its blast was mainly concussion, making it most effective against armor and artillery, and the sandbag-lined bunkers of our NDP. The number of RPGs we found that day was astounding, and proved that the enemy we faced was better equipped than we had thought.

Rocket Propelled Grenade (RPG).

The enemy's uniforms, complete with insignia and pith helmets, confirmed we were up against hard core units of the Viet Cong and North Vietnamese Army, not just the black pajama clad Viet Cong from our battle earlier in October.

We made our way back to the foxholes before nightfall, sat around the holes and ate our C rations. We started discussing what we had been through that day, sharing stories of what we experienced on our way up Hill 203. The strain was apparent on everyone's faces, and we were extremely exhausted. Several young men from the South Vietnamese special forces unit came over to my hole, and sat down as we all cleaned our weapons. We shared our food with them, but could not talk, for none of us spoke each other's language. I pulled out my wallet and showed them pictures of Sally, and patted them on the back, thanking them for such a hard fought battle earlier in the day. I believe they understood my intentions, if not my words. The next day, an artillery battery was airlifted in our perimeter, in the clearing of the forest between Delta Company and Charlie Company on our left. Two things suddenly became apparent with the arrival of these 105mm howitzers: First, our battalion commanders felt we needed reenforcements, based on the number of enemy we had seen the last two days, and secondly, we knew the enemy would do everything in his power to break through our perimeter to capture these weapons. The sight of the artillery, therefore, was reassuring and frightening.

The next two days, however, were calm and uneventful. Patrols found nothing more than deserted base camps, just the opposite of our frustrating patrols in Operation Shenandoah, which ended in ambushes. The date was November 1, and I looked forward to chalking off another month in my twelve-month tour. The band around my helmet had all twelve months inked in, and I crossed off the fourth month of my time in Vietnam. It was late in the afternoon, and mail call had just been completed. We all sat around our holes reading words from home. I received a care package from Sally's roommate, Linda Tieman, which contained two dozen chocolate chip cookies. They disappeared within minutes as soon as the rest of the squad saw them. Diehl was out on LP (listening post—a two- to four-man unit which is placed about fifty meters to the front of each rifle company, to listen for enemy movement. If the enemy approached, they would return to the perimeter to warn us of an attack).

James Chavis, Steve Diehl, and Terry Courange with captured North Vietnamese Army weapons and gear.

Fierro, Ciliberti, and I were getting ready to bed down in our hole, and begin guard duty for the night. Pritch, Freppon, and Haymon were in the hole to my right. Adams; Passantino, our medic; and our platoon leader, Lieutenant Gardner, were on our left.

After two peaceful days of patrolling, we felt the battle was over, and that we would be airlifted out soon to find the enemy. But as always, before night fell we placed our trip flares and claymore mines out to our front, which was a daily duty in a war zone. Only six weeks in the field, and we felt we were experienced, seasoned fighters now. On Delta Company's side of the perimeter, the trenches and rubber trees were perpendicular to our foxholes, meaning that the rows of trees and trenches approached straight to our front, requiring us to fill the trenches with enough trip flares and claymores should the enemy try to use the trenches to infiltrate our NDP.

About ten o'clock, Fierro and I were sitting quietly in the still darkness of the forest as Ciliberti slept, when suddenly the night was shattered by explosions all around us. Immediately, everyone began shouting and running for cover, as the mortars poured down from the sky. The foliage of the trees prevented any moon or starlight from reaching the forest, and sounds were audible all over the perimeter, as they bounced off the dense leaves above our heads. Once again the hollow thump of the mortar explosions sent shivers down my spine, and all three of us dove into the hole. Watching the explosions light up the forest was like seeing a lightning blast—from total darkness to blinding light, and ear shattering blasts. We could tell that the area where the mortars were falling was in the clearing, where the artillery battery was located. The enemy had recorded our positions well, and was doing his best to eliminate the howitzers. Fortunately for us, they failed that night. We remained in our holes throughout the barrage, which lasted about an hour, and slowly died down. We then crawled out of the holes, and prepared for what we knew was to follow—a ground attack, standard military tactics for the Viet Cong and North Vietnamese. We sat there, weapons loaded and trained on the darkness to our front, but nothing came. We sat there for two hours, with no one talking. Just whispers, and the sound of rifle bolts and ammunition clips being filled. I felt the enemy was doing this purposefully, making us sweat and feel the fear building up inside.

Sometime after midnight, the listening post suddenly detonated their claymore mines, and came running back to the perimeter. Because of the darkness, Diehl accidentally jumped in my hole, and frantically yelled "They're coming. They're coming in. Lots of them." Once again we heard shouts of "Get ready. Keep your eyes open." There were about three hundred of us in the NDP, and we had no idea of the size of the force about to attack. Outside of the metallic sounds of rifles and ammunition, silence once again took over the darkness as we anxiously waited.

Suddenly, trip flares lit up all around the perimeter, and the enemy was illuminated, as if he came out of nowhere. All the weapons around the perimeter exploded in unison, as the assault on the NDP began. It was evident from the first few minutes that the main enemy force was attacking on the other side of the perimeter, in front of Alpha Company. The trip flares to our front decreased almost as suddenly as they began, and there was nothing we could do but stay in our holes, and keep watch to the front, as explosions and rifle and machine gun fire roared behind us on the other side. Another enemy tactic was unfolding in this battle. The VC and NVA usually attack at night in one direction against the NDP; there could be multiple assaults in one night, as they tried to find a weak spot in the perimeter. This attack started with Alpha Company.

After an hour, the enemy pulled back, and darkness, and silence, again descended upon us. The silence was stressful, because we all thought to ourselves, where would the next attack occur? I was too nervous to just sit there, so I took some C rations out of my back pack, and began to eat a can of pears, accompanied with some warm Kool-Aid in my canteen. I laid the canteen on the roof of sandbags in front of me. Tonight we were not fighting from inside the holes. With four of us, we knelt behind the foxhole, and were shooting over the roof. After finishing off the pears, I tossed the empty can into the trench to my right, just over the wall of sandbags. On the other side of this wall was our 90mm rocket launcher, several of which were placed around the perimeter in case of an overwhelming ground attack. Its presence was reassuring and intimidating at the same time. A stack of rockets lie next to it just behind the wall to my right.

Around two o'clock in the morning, shortly after I finished my can of pears, we started hearing strange sounds to our front. We soon knew that another attack was coming, and this time, directly in front of Delta Company. We heard voices of the enemy as he approached our side of the perimeter in the darkness. I could hear plainly their voices in Vietnamese, apparently officers shouting orders to the troops. Whistles were blowing, bolts of rifles and machine guns clicking, leaves rustling, and twigs snapping under the feet of the approaching soldiers. They did not try to keep their approach quiet or secretive, which unnerved me immensely. I was more fearful in these brief moments than I had ever been, knowing that enemy soldiers were out there in the darkness, and I would soon meet their full force. I grabbed my ammo belt, and stacked all of my twenty magazines on the sandbags to my right, for easy access, knelt down in a firing position, pointed my rifle in the direction of the voices in the darkness, and waited.

We didn't have to wait long. Suddenly the trip flares we placed on the ground in front of our foxholes burst out all along the perimeter, illuminating the rows of rubber trees, our positions, and the oncoming soldiers. They wore two different uniforms—one khaki, and the other green, both with pith helmets—the 271st Viet Cong Regiment and 165th North Vietnamese Army. We detonated our claymores, which took out two or three soldiers at a time, and starting throwing flares and grenades at them as they approached. The whole perimeter opened up, but the attack was clearly in front of Delta Company. I fired my M-16 like I had never fired it before, mostly on full automatic. I was sitting in a pool of hot empty shells, as they cascaded out of my rifle. Diehl was to my direct left, and firing his M-14 automatic rifle. Ciliberti had the M-79 grenade launcher, and was firing right in the midst of the soldiers just twenty or so meters away. Fierro was on my far left, firing his M-16. My rifle starting smoking again, but I kept firing, loading new magazines about every two or three minutes. At one point Diehl tapped me on the shoulder, pointing to a rifle flash coming from behind a tree to my right in the darkness, signaling that there was one or more soldiers there in a fortified position. We had to eliminate it. I loaded a fresh clip, pointed at the flash, and fired on full automatic, emptying my clip of the twenty rounds. The flash disappeared.

The fighting was so heavy at first that I didn't recognize the jet fighters that were dive bombing along our side of the perimeter, dropping their payload less than one hundred meters to our front. Artillery shells were also coming in, exploding in the same area, right on top of the charging enemy soldiers. It was then that I felt the shrapnel and dirt from the blasts, falling down on our helmets and sandbags. We knew we were in trouble, with so much close-up artillery and bombing support. I could see tracers dancing up into the sky, as the enemy soldiers tried to hit the jets as they swooped down upon them. The darkness of the forest was lit up with tracers—red, green, and white—bouncing off trees and the ground, ricocheting in all directions. It was an unreal sight. The smell of gunpowder and napalm thickened the air around us, and the noises were deafening. The colors and madness of the tracers, and din of the explosions, created a surreal scene of hell in front of us, but we had no time to comprehend its ugliness. We had to keep shooting directly to our front, as the enemy kept coming at us.

Lieutenant Gardner, from his hole to my left, yelled to us to make sure there were no enemy soldiers in the trench, which wound its way into the perimeter between my foxhole and Pritch's to my right. Since I was nearest the trench, I was ordered to crawl over the wall on my right, and secure it with rifle fire. I acknowledged that the claymores we set up were all detonated, so we had to secure it ourselves. I jumped over the three-foot wall, threw in a couple of grenades, and emptied another clip into the trench. I could not see anything, but I felt that if anyone was there, they were now dead. I then crawled back to the wall, and jumped over it to the safety of our hole.

Throughout the fight, we could hear bullets as they passed over our heads, and the green and white tracers which illuminated them. When they buzzed by, they made a popping sound, like miniature missiles breaking the sound barrier. I glanced at the wall of sandbags in front and on top of our foxhole, and could see from the flares that they were riddled to bits, the dirt slowly leaking through the bullet holes. I realized that we were just inches from being killed. We also heard the woosh of RPG rounds as they passed over the holes, most of which were exploding in the trees around us. One clear hit on our hole and the four of us would be dead. We made good targets because the number of trip flares, hand thrown flares, and explosions, illuminated our holes for the enemy to see. *Can't think such thoughts,* I said to myself. *Got to keep fighting.*

Ciliberti ran out of grenades, so Diehl, Fierro, and I kept on shooting as the attack got closer. Our targets were clear to us from the light of the flares, so clear, in fact, that I was on one knee, firing my M-16, using the rifle sight at the end of the barrel, clearly seeing my targets. Because of that, the only section of my body that was exposed to my right was my shoulder, since I was behind a three-foot wall, and the right side of my face was protected by my helmet as I peered through the rifle sight. Suddenly there was an ear-shattering explosion just over the wall, not more than three or four meters away. An RPG had exploded just over the wall, destroying the 90mm rocket launcher. The blast threw me into my buddies on the left, and I tumbled to the ground behind them. I immediately shouted that I was hit, and I looked up at Diehl and Ciliberti, and Diehl shouted "1-6, 1-6 . . . come here. Man down." The code 1-6 meant to summon the medic. We didn't want to let the enemy know when we needed a medic, for they, themselves, were targets to enemy fire.

I was on my back, and when I peered down at my right shoulder, I saw nothing. I thought I had lost my arm. It was bent back behind me, and I had no feeling in the arm. The right side of my uniform had been torn away by the blast, and all I could see was blood, as it flowed out of my shoulder. I remember feeling how warm it was. Ciliberti was on his hands and knees, holding me down, saying "You're going to be OK Fee, the medic's coming." I thought at that moment that "time out" should be called. My world suddenly was upside down. Diehl and Fierro were "still in the game," but there I was, on the ground, and for a split second I thought everything should stop for me.

I was looking up at the rubber trees above, and the white sap from the wounded trees was pouring down like rain, covering the four of us with its sticky substance. It took just a few minutes for Frank Passantino, our platoon medic, to crawl over to our hole. As soon as he leapt over the wall, Ciliberti grabbed my M-16, and began firing to the front. From my vantage point, I could not tell how the battle was going. Passantino ripped off my shirt, pulled my

Frank Passantino, Delta Company's medic.

limp right arm from behind my back, and laid it on my stomach, saying "You're OK, Fee. You still have your arm." I had no feeling in the arm, and it was grossly swollen about double its size. I saw two gaping holes in my shoulder, with blood flowing out from each. Passantino took bandages from his pouch, and began to wrap my shoulder as tightly as he could. He asked if I wanted morphine, and I replied "Hell yes!" As he broke open the glass vial, and jabbed both ends into my left arm, he turned to me, almost with a smile, and said "Fee, this is the first time I've given morphine, lying on my back, bullets flying overhead in the middle of the night." Recognizing his attempt to calm and humor me, I replied "What a treat!"

Passantino then pulled me over to a tree directly behind the foxhole, and sat me in a sitting position, with Ciliberti, Fierro and Diehl directly to my front. I looked at my watch, and it was shortly after three o'clock in the morning. I knew that I would have to wait for a medical airlift out of the battle, and felt there was no way they would be able to fly into the perimeter in the middle of the night with so much fighting going on. Passantino took a 45-caliber pistol out of his holster, wrapped my left hand around the handle, and laid it on my stomach. "You'll need this more than me," he said, "I gotta run." And with those words, he jumped over the wall toward another foxhole to my left, where Willie Carson lay wounded with enemy machine gun fire in his belly.

    I grew thirsty, a natural result of my loss of blood. I yelled to Ciliberti to toss me my canteen, but he said that all the Kool-Aid was gone. The RPG blast which exploded next to me started a fire, and with a pile of 90mm rockets close by, Ciliberti had used my canteen to help extinguish the fire. I would have to remain thirsty.

    The fighting went on, as I lay there and watched my three buddies continue to fire to the front, throwing grenades and flares at the charging enemy. The morphine started to do its job, and my pain started to subside. I began to grow dizzy, but never lost consciousness. The noise was still deafening, but seemed to grow more distant. The visual madness of the explosions and ricocheting bullets were vividly there in front of me, but I felt removed from the danger. I picked up the Saint Christopher medal hanging around my neck, which Sally had given to me before I left for Vietnam, and read the words engraved on the back "Lovingly Sally." I knew I was in trouble, and for the first time, I felt I might die. I tried to think about how I could survive until morning, or get through the battle, whichever occurred first, and get on that helicopter. But I sensed that I would not make it. The hour of the night, and the intensity of the fighting, would prohibit my being airlifted out. I had never been in a more helpless situation.

At that moment, I peered up into the trees above, illuminated brightly by the colors of the battle, and saw a face. I recognized this face. It was Sally's father, who had died in September. Despite the din of the battle, I heard his voice say to me, *You are going to be all right.* After those words, the face disappeared. I did not understand what had just happened, but I felt the impact of those words, and an inner peace settled over me. *I have just seen an angel,* I thought to myself.

Shortly before four o'clock the battle seemed to wane. There was less fighting, and I thought that the enemy had been driven back. I sat there in silence, watching my buddies who were no longer firing at such a frenzied pace. A few minutes later Sergeant Page and Frank Passantino walked to our hole, and told me I was getting out of there. "No way," I said, "It's four o'clock in the morning!" Passantino said "Never mind . . . come with us." I was able to walk, barely, with both men holding me steady, one on each side. It was still dark, and we arrived at a clearing to our left, where Charlie Company was positioned. I started getting faint, and Passantino laid me down on the ground. I asked for water, but he said he couldn't allow that because of my wounds. I looked around and saw several other wounded men, from Delta and Charlie Company, all lying on their backs. "Doc" told me the colonel had convinced some brave souls to fly in now, during the battle, instead of waiting until morning. He said Willie Carson and I would be the first to be airlifted out.

I watched the first Huey helicopter come in and land in the clearing. Immediately, Passantino helped me over to the side of the chopper, and threw me onto the floor. Two other men carried Carson on a stretcher, and laid him next to me. There were two soldiers on the chopper, and they said "Keep your head down. They'll be shooting at us." I was good at following orders. I yelled to Passantino that I would see him when I returned. He agreed, and pounded the floor, signaling the pilot to take off. As we ascended into the night sky, I peered over the edge of the floor and gazed down at the fighting below. The perimeter was clearly outlined in the darkness by the flares being thrown out toward the charging enemy. I could also see explosions all across the perimeter from the artillery barrage, and jets were still dropping their deadly arsenal all along the perimeter. Green and white tracers were climbing into the sky, in the enemy's futile attempts to down the jets. The scene indeed was more frightful, almost surreal, from the protected perch of this altitude, as opposed to the perspective of a grunt in the hole, with bullets and RPGs racing directly at you. I thought about Fierro, Diehl, and Ciliberti, down in that rubber tree hell, still in extreme danger from the battle. I said to myself that I would return to them someday, and prayed for their survival.

Danger Forward continued the narrative of the battle.

This two hour period was one of the most colorful of the war. From their NDP, the "Swamp Rats" saw the sky alternately illuminated by flares, artillery and mortar shells, rockets and bombs. The downward parabolas of red tracers from the supporting gunships were matched by those curving upward from the enemy's heavy machine guns. And far from ceasing when airstrikes were brought in, the enemy gunners let go with bursts of fire at the low swooping jets.

As the helicopter ascended to a safe altitude in its escape from the battle, I lay down on the floor of the Huey, and stared at Carson, who appeared seriously wounded. A medic was nursing his stomach wounds, while another soldier was holding a bottle of plasma in the air. As I watched the lights from the villages below pass by, I then fell off into a short, troubled sleep.

Following the battle, *Danger Forward* wrote,

> The highlight of Shenandoah II was, of course, the battle for Loc Ninh. On 5 November after a combined total of nearly 1,000 enemy soldiers had been killed at Loc Ninh by US and ARVN units, General Hay (1st Division Commander) escorted the press through the "Dogface" NDP. Before a gathering of 22 correspondents, he remarked: "The courage and professionalism of the Big Red One soldiers leaves nothing to be desired. They truly are a credit to the Army and the nation." Shortly after this General Westmoreland pronounced the victory as one of the greatest of the entire war, and sent his congratulations to the men of the First Division.

CHAPTER 5

Aftermath

"my days in the military soon would be over"

LOOKING BACK ON THE NIGHT OF NOVEMBER 1, 1967, I consider my evacuation from the battle of Loc Ninh a miracle. An extraordinary set of circumstances took place that night which, if one or two had not occurred, I would not be here today. First, the attack. As I described earlier, my firing position was such that the only exposed part of my body to the RPG blast was my right shoulder. Had I not been looking through the rifle sight, had I not had on my helmet, my head would have been blown away, or at least my face would have received the full extent of the explosion. Secondly, Colonel Cavazos (who retired from the U.S. Army as a four star general) told me at one of the Delta Company reunions, years after the war, that I was not airlifted out of the battle by a Red Cross or medical helicopter. Medical personnel were not required to fly into battle zones at night; the missions were considered too dangerous, and guarding against the risk of further death, and loss of helicopters, was deemed more important than evacuating the wounded on the ground. At Loc Ninh, we began to run low on ammunition for our M-16s, automatic rifles, and M-79 grenade launchers. Ciliberti had, in fact, depleted his supply of grenades from our hole that night. Colonel Cavazos ordered resupply helicopters to our NDP at three o'clock in the morning, and as they arrived, he ordered them grounded until the wounded from that night's battle were safely on board. I was one of those fortunate men who made it out of that battleground hell that night, thanks to the heroic leadership of our battalion commander, and the courageous, selfless sacrifices that those helicopter pilots demonstrated at the battle of Loc Ninh.

Third, my vision of an angel. I have shared this experience only with select members of my immediate family, but rewriting these memoirs forty-five years later, I feel compelled to share it with a wider circle. Perhaps because of my age, my retirement, and my first grandchild I have mellowed my resistance to keeping this vision a secret. I barely knew Sally's father, and had met him only several times. We certainly had no relationship, no feelings for each other, which would have occupied space in my brain to make him appear to me while I was faced with imminent danger. I was fully conscious throughout the experience, although sedated, and the battle was in full force, with extreme levels of noise and visual distractions from the explosions, tracers, and soldiers fighting. But throughout it all, I remember seeing his face clearly. I count myself very fortunate, not only because I survived a near brush with death, but because my belief in God is bolstered not just by faith, but by knowledge. I do not have to rely solely on faith to know that there is life after death. I have seen it.

After my evacuation, we first flew to Quon Loi, just about a half hour away, where we patrolled a few weeks earlier. The division had set up a triage station under several tents, where the wounded coming in from the field were met by medical personnel, and divided into two groups; those whose wounds were superficial would be attended to and bedded down at Quon Loi, and return to the field as soon as they were well. The more seriously wounded would again board helicopters and be flown to Long Binh, outside Saigon, where the First Division maintained the 93rd Evacuation Hospital.

After our chopper landed at Quon Loi, I was walked over to a tent packed with wounded soldiers, some on stretchers, others lying on the ground, or propped up against trees and tent poles. The tent was overflowing with wounded, which told me the Big Red One battalions were locked in a fierce battle with the enemy on this night. I was on the ground, sitting up against a stump or tree trunk, and started to get dizzy. A medic came over to check my wounds, and changed my badly bloodied bandages. He told me that I would be medivaced out to Long Binh as soon as a helicopter was available. As I lay there, an older gentleman came over to me, and introduced himself as a chaplain. We chatted for a few moments about where we came from, and quite honestly, I was never more disinterested in discourse at that moment. Thankfully, a medic soon came by to accompany me to a waiting helicopter, and confirmed I was headed to Long Binh.

It was a short ride, and too soon we were on a helipad, where a team of nurses and medics raced out to help us off the choppers. My arrival was greeted by exams, shots, washings, X-rays, more shots, and prep for surgery. I had persevered through an hour of pre-op exams, and as I was standing on a scale to be weighed, I finally fainted, for the first time, from loss of blood. The doctors at Long Binh informed me a few days later that I had lost half my body's blood, and that had I, indeed, remained on the battlefield for just a few hours more, I would not have survived.

When I woke up from my fainting spell, I was lying buck naked on a stretcher in an operating room, with an army issue olive drab towel draped over my privates. I gazed up at the most beautiful sight I had seen since leaving the states in June, four months earlier—an army nurse leaning over me, wiping my head with a wet towel, softly asking if I needed anything, and assuredly telling me I was going to be all right. Her hair was cropped short, and though she was in army fatigues, she might as well have worn a bikini. She was beautiful. While cleaning the blood and mud from my face, neck, and shoulders she noticed the Saint Christopher medal around my neck. Military procedure called for religious items like necklaces or bracelets to remain on the body during surgery, so it was necessary for the nurse, after cleaning the medal, to tape it to my left shoulder, to keep it out of the way during surgery. She glanced at the inscription on the back of the medal, which read "Lovingly Sally," and asked, "Who's Sally?" Without a whiff of guilt or betrayal, I almost convinced myself to respond that she was my mother. Fortunately, I had not lost too much consciousness to remain faithful to Sally, and told the truth.

Shortly, thereafter, I collapsed into a deep sleep as the operation on my shoulder began.

My stay at Long Binh was short. I woke up the day after my operation, wrapped in a body cast from my neck to my waist. My right arm was folded in front of my torso, under the cast, with my right hand sticking out through a hole in the front. The cast was tight, and it was hard to breathe. My right shoulder, the location of my wound, was wrapped in bandages, so the medics could access the wound, and clean it several times a day. The doctors informed me that the RPG blast completely shattered my right shoulder, and there was nothing left of the joint. I was scheduled for a second operation in a day or two to assess if a shoulder prosthesis was possible. This was 1967, and prosthetic joints were still rare, especially for the shoulder; the first operation was simply to explore the extent of the damage, and the second would begin the process of rebuilding what was left of the bones forming the shoulder—the humerus, clavicle, and scapula.

The day after my first operation, I remained drowsy, and sick from the anesthesia. An army major came over to my bed, and pinned a Purple Heart on my pillow while I was still semiconscious. He leaned over, taking my left hand in his, and whispered things about military pride and duty, and said "Job well done," which was the last thing I wanted to hear at that moment. He then dutifully went on to the next bed for a similar, personal ceremony.

I remained at Long Binh for five days, undergoing two operations on my shoulder, and remained in a full body cast throughout that week. The hospital was just a few miles from our base camp at Di An, and since there were other soldiers from Delta company among the wounded at the hospital, I had some visitors. The most senior officer among the wounded from our company was Top Sergeant King, who had a head wound, and I remember one day he came to my bed, walking on crutches, with a number of the men from "the rear" at Di An— the clerks, logistics, and supply soldiers of the First Division. These men were affectionately called "REMFs," which stands for "rear echelon mother fuckers." Even though we may have mildly disdained them while we were in the field in combat, deep down we admired and longed for such a position. During their visit, they gave us the latest information about the battle at Loc Ninh, taking place eighty miles to the north. They reported

Frank Puente (left), my replacement in Delta Company, and Bill Johnson. Puente made it home to Detroit, and we remain good friends. Johnson was killed by an RPG in April 1968.

that the battle had ended, with huge losses for the enemy. The enemy forces—Viet Cong and North Vietnamese—had undertaken a large, coordinated attack against the First Infantry Division, planning for a strategic victory prior to the Tet Offensive in January. But to the contrary, the battle resulted in overwhelming losses for the enemy; they had staged human wave attacks against three Big Red One battalions, and were repulsed in each engagement. There were reports of fighting so close, that in one fight, the 105mm howitzers were lowered to point blank range, with fuses cut for early detonation, so the blasts could decimate the charging soldiers. The REMFs told me that on Hill 203, where we led our assault a few days earlier, intelligence reports documented between 200 and 250 freshly dug enemy bunkers on the hill, demonstrating the determination and depth of the enemy we faced at Loc Ninh. I was also told that on November 2, the night after I was wounded, the enemy had broken through our perimeter, and tried to reach Colonel Cavazos's headquarters with a band of men armed with flamethrowers. They were killed before they completed their mission, but the battle demonstrated how serious this fight was.

Time Magazine reported about Loc Ninh, in its November 17, 1967, edition.

> At Loc Ninh, two enemy regiments that tried to overrun an Allied position (the 1st/18th) only nine miles from the Cambodian border, failed disastrously despite their proximity to frontier safety. By this week the Loc Ninh body count of North Vietnamese dead had grown to 926; U.S. intelligence estimated that perhaps half that many again had been dragged away for burial by their comrades, and that another 2,000 to 3,000 had been wounded. This high casualty rate (nearly 50%) for the two ill-fated Red regiments, who were ordered to take

the town at all costs, made Loc Ninh one of the war's most significant Allied victories."

After five days at Long Binh, I was shipped to the 106th Army General Hospital in Yokohama, Japan. From there, a month and another operation later, I arrived in the United States, at Fort Dix, New Jersey, on December 8, 1967. I had left for Vietnam in June, not expecting to be home until July of 1968, but had just completed an abbreviated four month tour in country, grateful to be home. I was home on leave for Christmas—an unbelievable, unforgettable reunion with my family and friends.

Doctors told me my days in the military soon would be over. After the Christmas holiday in 1967, I was stationed at the Valley Forge General Hospital, in Phoenixville, Pennsylvania, for the remainder of my service. One more operation in March (my fourth) confirmed earlier decisions by surgeons not to install a shoulder prosthesis; two much destruction of the three

At home on leave for Christmas 1967, with my brother Bob. I had graduated from a full body cast to a sling.

bones—the scapula, clavicle, and humerus—on which to build a good foundation. In my final operation, the bones were fused together, and while I had no shoulder joint, I could move my lower arm, a result on which doctors and patient were happy to agree. Receiving my medical discharge in August 1968, after ten months of hospitalization, I returned home, and enrolled in the University of Cincinnati the following month to resume college.

When I returned home, my body was thirty pounds lighter, and I had aged more than the four months I spent in Vietnam. I left for the war at age nineteen, spent my twentieth birthday on the USNS *Geiger* in the middle of the Pacific Ocean, and saw more in the next four months than I would experience for the rest of my life. The combined experiences of combat, exhaustion, losing close friends, and a near brush with death, matured me beyond my years. That four month period has become the focal point of my life, and I measure all challenges, fears, and sacrifices through the lens of what I once experienced in Vietnam. I am thankful for the experience, and have no regrets about my military service. Through it I have learned to value friendship, love, the simple pleasures of life, and life itself, much more than I would have without the hardships I faced. I am fortunate to have life, a wife, children, and one granddaughter. I try to imagine how they would all disappear had I not survived the night of November 1, 1967, at Loc Ninh; and it is then that I just want to hug them, and thank them for bringing meaning to my life. I am blessed.

Happiness Is...Having A Son Home From Vietnam

Happiness for the Robert Fee family is having their son, Bill, home from Vietnam.

The house at 6830 Sampson Ln., Silverton, is filled with merriment. Gone is the apprehension that hung like a cloud while Bill was in battle in Vietnam.

And even though he has two years of a three-year hitch to serve, his fighting days are over ...the hard way, for Bill caught a rocket blast in his right shoulder at the battle of Loc Ninh Nov. 2. He was a rifleman with the First Infantry Division.

"I was evacuated by helicopter and spent a month and a half in hospital there." He's undergoing treatment for his immobilized shoulder at Valley Forge Hospital, Pa. and is home on a 30-day convalescent leave.

Bill, a 1965 graduate of Walnut Hills High School, decided to enlist while a sophomore in Business Administration at UC. Not only did he enlist in the infantry, but he volunteered for Vietnam duty. "I wanted to do my part and I don't regret my decision. It was a very maturing experience."

WILLIAM FEE
...Best Christmas Present

What is this veteran's opinion of Vietniks? "They couldn't hurt morale in Vietnam any more than they have by their protests of the war. Otherwise morale is high."

Cincinnati Enquirer *article, Christmastime 1967.*

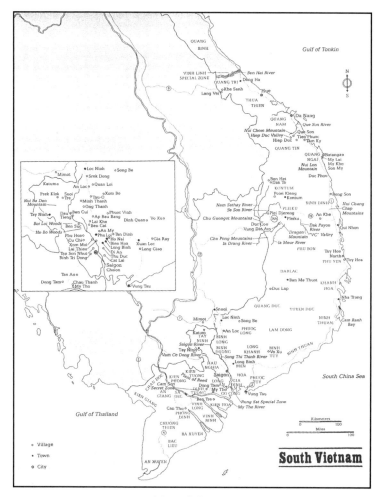

Map of Vietnam

CHAPTER 6

Coping with Vietnam

"The general has been the glue"

FORTY-FIVE YEARS HAVE PASSED, as of this writing, since I originally wrote the story of my months in Vietnam. The memoirs were written from my hospital bed in the Valley Forge General Hospital, where I spent the last eight months of my military service, undergoing a fourth operation to rebuild my shoulder, still without a prosthesis. The original memoirs were typed on an old Royal typewriter, were never published, and placed in a folder along with some newspaper clippings about Delta Company's exploits in the Vietnam War in 1967. Until recently, the whole file only gathered dust.I undertook the revision of the memoirs because I have been blessed to experience a lifetime of friendship with a few of my buddies from Delta Company. One must remember that, unlike the soldiers returning from the wars in Iraq and Afghanistan, the Vietnam veteran faced a range of acceptance at home which ranged from indifference to open

Bill and Sally. Home for good – August 1968.

hostility. The late 1960s brought violence and protests against the war into the streets, on campuses, and dominated the headlines. The returning soldiers were the only tangible, visible, targets against which the violence turned. It was an ugly time to be a Vietnam veteran, and it hurt even more when our military service and sacrifice was despised and denigrated. In the 1970s many Vietnam vets found themselves once again in a strange land—unwanted, uncared for, and wrongfully blamed for losing the war. Hollywood did its best to add to the fictionalized denigration of the Vietnam veterans; movies released in the late 1970s over dramatized and stigmatized the veterans as deranged, unstable, and murderous. Think *Coming Home* and *Deer Hunter*. The public's perception of, and hostility toward Vietnam veterans fed the personal turmoil this generation of young soldiers suffered. I was discharged in August 1968, and began my classes at the University of Cincinnati in September. During the first of week of classes, I vividly remember wearing my Vietnam jungle shirt, proudly displaying the Big Red One patch on my right sleeve. After my first day, I never wore it again on campus. I was reviled, jeered at, ridiculed, and despised, not by my friends, but by strangers. I was confused and bewildered, not comprehending the juxtaposition of my Vietnam experiences with my new life as a civilian. This was the beginning of a long, slow downward spiral of emotions and self confidence.

Complicating the isolation and depression returning veterans experienced was the military's practice of sending soldiers to Vietnam, primarily combat infantrymen, as single replacements to rifle companies in the field. These young men went to Vietnam alone, joined a seasoned and battle weary group of soldiers already in combat, and returned home alone, often just days after being pulled from the field. A tragic number of these men faced a hostile, uncaring world upon their return home, feeding the anxieties that a return to civilian life would bring.

The toll on me was more muted, because I went to Vietnam with a group of men with whom I had trained, had a family that stood by me, friends who welcomed me home, and a girlfriend who stayed with me throughout the twenty months I served in the army, and whom I married a year after being discharged. However, I began to fall victim to my own demons from the war in 1974, undergoing depression, an overwhelming urge for solitude and isolation, which ended in a divorce three years later. My depression had ruined my marriage; it was all my fault, and yet I could not understand why I was obsessed with wanting to be alone. I visited three psychiatrists for my depression, yet none of them had a diagnosis, nor a remedy for why I was feeling lonely, depressed, and even suicidal. Post traumatic stress disorder, as it's now called, was yet to be defined for the returning soldiers from Vietnam in the early 1970s, and I spent four years in a struggle to find normalcy and peace in my life.

I finally did in 1978. During those dark days, I spent hours talking in a mirror in my apartment, telling myself that I would get better. I had survived the worst of circumstances as a twenty-year-old rifleman in Vietnam, came preciously close to death, endured ten months in three army hospitals, underwent four operations, and finally a medical discharge. I spent hours in front of that mirror convincing myself that my life was not over, that I could rebuild a life with my wife, if she would have me back, and start life anew.

I was extremely fortunate. I had crawled out of my depression by myself, with psychiatrists just shaking their heads and shrugging their shoulders, and even though I had ruined my marriage, I was committed to rebuilding my life with Sally. We remarried the following year, in August of 1978, and made three promises to form the foundation for our second marriage—I would build a career, not just exist in a job; we would buy our first house; and start a family. Just two months after our remarriage, I was fortunate to start a new career with WCPO-TV, a career which spanned thirty-two years. The following month

Sally and I bought our first house. And just over one year later our first child, Emily, was born. Our son, Evan, was born twenty-two months later. We had accomplished all three goals.

Another reason for this second edition of my memoirs is due to the contact I maintained with a small group of soldiers from Delta Company, beginning in 1985, which continues to this day, and has allowed the luxury of learning new details about our battles from our officers, and from archives and publications which have enriched the account of the first edition, all of which I did not have at my disposal in 1968.

I have been extremely fortunate to have as my closest friends the group of young men with whom I fought in Vietnam, two who saved my life—General Cavazos and my medic, Frank Passantino. On several occasions I have visited Ron Campsey (East Quogue, New York), Frank Passantino (Flushing, New

First contact with Delta Company veterans took place in July 1985 in East Quogue, New York. Pictured from the left are Mike Ciliberti, Steve Pritchett, James Chavis, Ron Campsey, Steve Diehl, and Bill Fee.

York), Mike Ciliberti (Lake Wylie, South Carolina), Edgar Ruble (Chicago, Illinois), Frank Puente (Dearborn, Michigan), and Gen. Richard Cavazos (Ret.) in San Antonio, Texas.

Included on my list of regular visits, in fact twice a year—Memorial Day and November 1—is Jack Freppon, who was killed on his second tour in Vietnam, on February 2, 1969, at age twenty. Jack received the Distinguished Service Cross for his valor in the battle in which he died. The DSC is the military's second highest honor, second only to the Medal of Honor. His DSC citation, dated April 23, 1969, reads,

> Sergeant Freppon was serving as point man when he was suddenly pinned to the ground by fragmentation, rocket propelled grenades and automatic weapons fire from well concealed North Vietnamese Army troops. Fearing that his men would be trapped by the devastating hostile fire, he stood up to warn them of the entrenched enemy. Then, with complete disregard for his safety, he charged through the fusillade toward a North Vietnamese bunker. Although he was wounded repeatedly, he continued his assault on the fortification. He succeeded in destroying the bunker, and was stopped only when he was mortally wounded by an enemy rocket propelled grenade. His courage and self sacrifice prevented many of his comrades from being killed or wounded.

I served as pall bearer in Jack's funeral, in February of 1969, and felt extremely guilty when meeting his parents for only the second time at his memorial service. When I looked into his mother's eyes, I felt inside that she was asking why it was not me, instead of her son, inside the casket. It was just my imagination, but one brought on my closeness with Jack in Vietnam, and

Jack Freppon's grave marker in Gate of Heaven Cemetery, Cincinnati, Ohio.

having to face his parents. Survival guilt began for me on that very sad day, and continued for many years. In some respects it will never go away.

When one experiences a life and death struggle, the thought of *Why not me* never goes away. Jack is buried in Gate of Heaven Cemetery in Cincinnati, and my visits are the fulfillment of a promise we made to each other at Loc Ninh—we would remain friends when we returned home, and would visit each other regularly. I have kept that promise every year, with visits to his grave on Memorial Day and November 1.

The boys of Delta Company, First Battalion, 18th Infantry, First Infantry Division, fought well in Vietnam. I was privileged to serve with them, and am blessed to this day to call them my friends. Delta Company has had three reunions—a twentieth in 1987, a fortieth in 2007, and a forty-fifth in 2012. Our gatherings are usually held in San Antonio, Texas, the home for General Cavazos. Throughout the years since we served together,

General Cavazos has provided a historical context to our battles, a perspective we had not the privilege to possess in 1967. The general has been the glue for our continued friendship and reunions. When we are together, he unashamedly showers love and admiration on "his boys." His letters to me are selfless, as if from a devoted father, and he goes out of his way to make all of the soldiers who served under his leadership feel like heroes. No doubt he knew the destructive forces at work on the Vietnam veterans in the 1970s, and his devotion, love, and friendship have done much to heal those mental wounds.

Delta Company's 40th reunion, November 2007, Hico, Texas. Gen. Richard Cavazos sitting in front row with black hat. To his right is Capt. Charles Carden, Delta Company commander. To his left, Second Platoon Lieutenant Melvin Bray.

Ronnie Campsey lives in East Quogue, New York, on Long Island, with his wife, Shana, and owns a restaurant there. It is a family affair, with his wife and kids all part of the operation. Ronnie has been the chronicler of Delta Company, and the leader in keeping us together as a group of friends following the

Bill Fee and Gen. Richard Cavazos, November 2007, Hico, Texas.

Frank Fierro, Mike Ciliberti, Bill Fee. Foxhole buddies at Loc Ninh, together again at Delta Company's 40th reunion, November 2007.

Frank Passantino, Delta Company's medic, who saved my life at Loc Ninh on November 1, 1967.

Gen. Cavazos, Joe Galloway, Bill Fee at the general's 80th birthday in San Antonio in January 2009. Joe Galloway was a reporter in Vietnam, covered the first combat between the U.S. Army (First Cavalry Division) and North Vietnamese forces in November 1965. He is coauthor of the book We Were Soldiers Once . . . and Young *with Col. Hal Moore, who led the operation. Joe and the general are very close.*

Sally Fee and General Cavazos at his 80th birthday celebration in San Antonio, January 2009.

war. He has been relentless in his tireless efforts at keeping us together and in communication with each other. In June of 2013, Ronnie Campsey's pictures from Vietnam, and some of his weapons and equipment, were installed in the First Infantry Division Museum in Wheaton, Illinois. Several of us joined Ron and Shana, and their daughter, Phoebe, for the dedication of the exhibit. Needless to say, this was a proud moment for all of us, and helped heal some of the scars from the memories of the 1970s.

Mike Ciliberti is retired, living in Lake Wylie, South Carolina. Steve Diehl lives in Erie, Pennsylvania, and is a retired postal carrier. Frank Passantino lives in Flushing, New York, with his lovely wife, Linda, and is a retired baker. Melvin Brav, one of Delta Company's lieutenants, lives in San Diego with his wife, Diana, and is a frequent attendee at our reunions. I visited Steve Pritchett in 1979 when he lived in Vancouver, Washington, and he stayed with Sally and me for a while in 1985, but I have lost track of him since. Frank Fierro lives in Artesia, New Mexico, with his wife, Mary Helen, and is still working. Frank Puente (Dearborn, Michigan), joined Delta Company following the battle at Loc Ninh, and has become my good friend as well, since he has attended two of our reunions. He will be married to Kathy MacDonald in July 2013.

Three Delta Company reunions, and a few smaller gatherings of veterans visiting General Cavazos in San Antonio, have blessed me beyond measure, and have allowed the memories of 1967 to finally kindle a warm place in my heart. When we are together, we often say "Brothers then, together again," not hiding our admiration and devotion to each other. The continued friendship, and especially the reunions, of this small group of Vietnam veterans have extinguished most of the survival guilt and any degree of sorrow which lingered within me during the 1970s. Having a life partner and wife, Sally, who experienced the sorrow, separation, and difficulties of coping after the war, has been my lifesaver. She has stood by me, silently supporting me through good times and bad, and is firmly entrenched with the family of Delta Company. I look back at these years of my youth as a blessing, an opportunity which afforded me a unique exposure to life and death, and one which has enriched me immensely with a perspective few others have experienced. I shall hold my friends, and my memories, deeply within my heart, for the remainder of my life.

APPENDIX

Letters Home

"I am proud to call you brother!"

> TUES. OCT. 31 (?)
>
> Dear Sweetheart,
>
> Time allows me to write just a little note. I'm sorry I haven't written for about 5 days, but I haven't had one free moment until now. We left Song Be real suddenly about four days ago and came to War Zone C, 5 miles below Quan Loi. In the past 3 days we've seen the heaviest fighting this battalion has ever experienced. I won't describe anything to you, I don't have time and I know you'd worry all the more. I doubt if I will even have a good chance to write until they lift us out of this location. Please bear with me, Sally, I love you and think of you, but there's no time to write. I don't know if you've seen anything in the newspapers or not, there's no publicity this time. I sure will be glad when this year is over, sweetheart, and I can once again be with you. Being with you seems like heaven, and right now it seems far, far away. I love you Sally — please think of me, I need you desperately. I'll write at first chance — you study hard and don't worry about writing. Most of all, bear with me, I'll be home about July, I'm living for that day. I love you.
>
> Bill

One of my last letters to Sally a day before I was wounded at Loc Ninh, November 1967.

THE AMERICAN NATIONAL RED CROSS

Thursday, 2 Nov '67

Dear Mom and Dad,

I do not know if you have been notified by the department of Army, but yesterday I was wounded. Now please don't worry, it is just a slight wound in the sholder and as soon as I am able to I will write you a letter.

Please tell Sally for me that I'm alright and as soon as I have enough strength I'll drop you a line. Once again, I'm alright and I'm in good hands.

Love,

Bill

P.S. For the moment I'm in the 93rd Evac Hospital at Long Binh.

B.

Letter dictated to the Red Cross, from which my parents were notified of my wound. They received it five days later.

THE VICE PRESIDENT
WASHINGTON

December 15, 1967

Dear Mr. and Mrs. Fee:

    A member of my staff recently visited many of our hospitalized GI's in Japan, Okinawa and The Philippines, as part of a special USO tour. The USO group included cartoonist Al Capp, columnist Art Buchwald, and author George Plimpton. They had an opportunity to visit with your son, William.

    I recently returned from Vietnam myself. Having also visited with many of our men there, I wanted you to know how proud we are of their sacrifices in the defense of democracy and freedom. This Nation, and free men everywhere, will be eternally in their debt.

Sincerely,

Hubert H. Humphrey

Mr. and Mrs. Robert Fee
6830 Sampson Lane
Cincinnati, Ohio

Letter to my parents from Vice-President Hubert Humphrey.

Thurs,
7 Dec 67

Hi Bill, well, I got your letter yesterday and I was real glad to hear from you. I almost cracked up when I saw your bloody shirt I thought for sure you were dying.

The night you & Willie got hit we were shooting like crazy and the next day we made a sweep and Bill, we (DELTA) (ALPHA) found an arsenal! 2 flamethrowers, about 14 AK 47's, 10 mach ine guns, carbines, web gear and a hell of a lot of those damn RPG's with hundreds of rounds. We captured 4 prisoners who said they were told to take (our hill) at all costs! We really kicked their ass Bill, you did your job, Bill, that's all anyone expects out of you. About 3 days after that, we pulled back to Quan Loi and I'm a Plt. Sgt.! Ha! Then I got a call from S-1 to get on a chopper for Di An. Now I'm on top of the "Black Virgin Mountain." Its pretty nice up here. Charlie doesn't even mess with us. I miss 3rd Sqd tho! Bill please keep in contact with me ok? My nerves were getting bad out where we were. We had a patrol about 2 days after you left, remember where we had the firefight? Well we went over that hill. There were freshly dug bunkers in the trenches and I mean at least 100-150!!! I (everyone) was really edgy! Well, Bill write whenever

Letter from Steve Pritchett, the first I heard from him following the battle of Loc Ninh.

Memoir of Vietnam, 1967

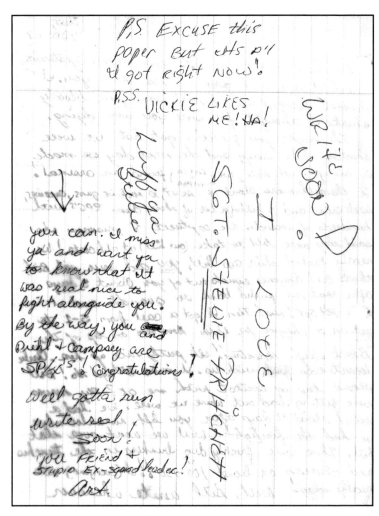

Back of letter from Steve Pritchett.

17 Nov '07

Dear Bill and Sally,

Just got the pictures and your letter. The framed picture sits right above on top of my desk -- a real treasure. More, I treasure your letter and words. You've got a real ability to touch one's soul. You're as close as any Band of Brothers. They mean so much because I saw your devotion, I saw you fight, I saw the hurt, all of which I committed you to. I thank God for the blessing all of you are. I am proud to call you brother!

Didn't mean to get so serious but where are the words to capture all that you mean to me. Live! Love, hold on to what you are, a credit to this country and to each other. Thank you, thank you! My warmest regards and affection to you both, Faithfully

Dick Cavazos

Letter from General Cavazos following our fortieth reunion in November 2007 in Hico, Texas. His words reveal the depth of his love for the men who served with him. His presence and devotion to us have helped heal our mental wounds throughout the years.

Index

A

Adams, George 18, 21, 38, 44, 45, 46, 59, 65, 66, 67, 73
American Traveler 42
Artesia, N.Mex. 108

B

battle of Loc Ninh, Vietnam 35, 60, 68, 83, 85, 86, 91, 92, 93, 103, 105, 106, 108, 110, 113
Best, 68
Bien Hoa, Vietnam 28
Big Red One 8, 13, 14, 22, 41, 43, 48, 50, 52, 58, 69, 83, 87, 91, 99
Brav, Diana 107
Brav, Melvin 58, 104, 107

C

C-130 military transport planes 28
California 18, 55
Cambodia 60

Cambodian border 1, 15, 25, 27, 29, 58, 59, 60, 91
Campsey, Phoebe 107
Campsey, Ronald 65, 66, 69, 101, 104, 107
Campsey, Shana 104, 107
Carden, Charles 35, 104
Carson, Willie 80, 81, 82
Cavazos, Richard 11, 14, 15, 27, 39, 44, 46, 49, 53, 56, 60, 61, 63, 64, 65, 67, 68, 69, 85, 86, 91, 101, 102, 103, 104, 105, 106, 107, 108, 115
Charlie (also, Victor Charlie or Viet Cong) 31, 56
Chavis, James 72, 101
Chicago, Ill. 102
Ciliberti, Mike 19, 20, 21, 36, 37, 44, 51, 72, 73, 76, 78, 79, 80, 82, 86, 101, 102, 105, 107
Cincinnati Reds 22
Cincinnati, Ohio 20, 22, 35, 68, 103
Courange, Terry 72

D

Danger Forward 48, 62, 69, 82, 83
Davidson, Shelby 19, 66, 67
Davis, Amos 35
Dearborn, Mich. 102, 108
Detroit, Mich. 90
Di An, Vietnam 10–14, 17–25, 27, 28, 32, 35, 37, 38, 45, 49, 51, 55, 60, 68, 89
  hospital 50
Diehl, Steve 19, 20, 21, 22, 37, 44, 45, 47, 51, 66, 71, 72, 74, 76, 78, 80, 82, 101, 107
Dien Bien Phu, Vietnam 28

E

East Quogue, N.Y. 101, 104
Erie, Pa. 107
European theater 13

F

Fee, Bill 19, 21, 33, 42, 78, 79, 98, 101, 105, 106
Fee, Bob 92
Fee, Sally (Isphording) 100, 101, 107, 108
Fierro, Frank 19, 20, 36, 37, 44, 45, 47, 51, 55, 68, 72, 73, 76, 78, 79, 82, 105, 108
Fierro, Mary Helen 108
First Infantry Division Museum 107
Flushing, N.Y. 101, 107
Fort Dix, N.J. 92
Fort Knox, Ky. 5, 7, 23
Fort Lee, Va. 5
Fort Lewis, Wash. 7, 14
Fort Polk, La. 5, 7, 14, 17
French 28
Freppon, Jack 19, 20, 22, 36, 44, 55, 66, 69, 72, 102, 103

G

Galloway, Joe 106
Gardner, Erle Stanley 21, 32
Gardner, Lt. 73, 77
Gate of Heaven Cemetery (Cincinnati) 103

H

Hay, General 48, 83
Haymon, Pete 19, 44, 50, 69, 73
Hico, Tex. 104, 105, 115
Hill 203 63, 64, 67, 69, 71, 91
Ho Chi Minh Trail 27

I

Iron Triangle 27
Isphording, Jean 32
Isphording, Mr. 35, 81, 86
Isphording, Sally 4, 7, 20, 21, 34, 35, 36, 37, 46, 47, 52, 55, 58, 62, 68, 71, 80, 81, 88, 98, 110

J

Johnson, Bill 90

K

King, "Top" 46, 89

L

Lai Khe, Vietnam 58
Lake Wylie, S.C. 102, 107
Loc Ninh, Vietnam 59, 62, 108
Long Binh, Vietnam 87, 88, 92
  hospital 89
Louisiana 17

M

MacDonald, Kathy 108
medals
  Distinguished Service Cross 69, 102
  Medal of Honor 102
  Purple Heart 89
Moore, Hal 106

N

New Mexico 55
93rd Evacuation Hospital 87
North Vietnamese 29, 56, 59, 65, 70, 72, 74, 91, 102, 106

O

106th Army General Hospital 92

165th North Vietnamese Army
    (NVA) 60, 62, 76
Operation Shenandoah 30, 41, 49,
    50, 53, 54, 56, 58, 71

P

Pacific Ocean 93
Page, Sgt. 22, 23, 81
Passantino, Frank 65, 73, 79, 80, 81,
    82, 101, 106, 107
Passantino, Linda 107
Perry Mason novels 21, 32
Phoenixville, Pa. 92
Phuoc Vinh, Vietnam 38, 41
Pritchett, Steve 18, 19, 21, 22, 24,
    25, 33, 37, 38, 44, 50, 51,
    55, 59, 68, 72, 77, 101,
    107, 113, 114
Puente, Frank 90, 102, 108
Puente, Kathy 108

Q

Quon Loi, Vietnam 25, 27, 28, 29,
    30, 33, 36, 38, 58, 60, 86,
    87

R

Red Cross 19, 24, 68, 85, 111
Ruble, Edgar 102
Rung Sat war zone 11

S

Saigon border 15
Saigon, Vietnam 1, 9, 11, 27, 87
San Antonio, Tex. 102, 103, 106,
    107, 108
San Diego, Calif. 107
Shenandoah II 83
Song Be, Vietnam 12, 37, 58
South Vietnam 1, 9, 27, 28, 30, 35
South Vietnamese 13, 28
    farmers 28
    montagnards 64, 66
    special forces 64, 71
Swamp Rats 1, 11, 14, 48, 82

T

Tacoma, Wash. 8

Tet Offensive 2, 60, 91
Tieman, Linda 71
Time Magazine 3
271st Viet Cong Regiment 42, 56,
    60, 76

U

uniforms 62
University of Cincinnati 2, 3, 20, 22,
    34, 35, 55, 93, 99
USNS *Geiger* 8, 9, 10, 93

V

Valley Forge General Hospital
    (Pa.) ix, 92, 97
Vancouver, Wash. 107
Victor Charlie (also, Charlie or Viet
    Cong) 31, 44
Viet Cong 13, 29, 42, 44, 45, 46, 47,
    49, 50, 51, 52, 53, 54, 56,
    59, 62, 64, 67, 69, 70, 74,
    91
    sackers 9
Viet Minh 56
Virginia 18, 38
Vung Tau, Vietnam 8, 9

W

War Zone C 1, 14, 15, 27, 41
wars
    Afghanistan 97
    Iraq 97
    Vietnam 97
    War of 1812 14
    World War I 13
    World War II 13, 56
*We Were Soldiers Once . . . and
    Young* (Galloway) 106
weaponry 30, 31, 34, 41, 45, 62, 63,
    65, 67, 68, 69, 70, 71, 72,
    74, 102
    105mm howitzers 71, 91
    45-caliber pistol 66, 80
    90mm rocket launcher 75, 78, 80
    AK-47 56, 66
    Chinese 56
    claymore mines 20, 48, 54, 73, 74,
    76, 77

M-14 19, 76
M-16 19, 29, 45, 46, 47, 56, 67,
    68, 76, 78, 79, 86
M-60 machine gun 44
M-79 grenade launcher 76, 86
RPG (rocket propelled
    grenade) 56, 65, 66, 70, 77,
    78, 80, 82
Russian 56
Westmoreland, General 83
Wheaton, Ill. 107

Y

Yokohama, Japan 92

About the Author

WILLIAM S. FEE served in Vietnam as a rifleman from July to November 1967 in Delta Company, 1st Battalion, 18th Regiment, First Infantry Division. He was wounded at the battle of Loc Ninh on November 1, and subsequently spent ten months in three army hospitals, undergoing four operations to repair his badly wounded shoulder. He was given a medical discharge from the army in August 1968. Fee wrote his first "Memoir" while a patient at the Valley Forge Army Hospital and revised it in 2013, adding details of his combat experience learned from Delta Company reunions and events of the years since he returned home. He spent most of his career working in the television industry, including thirty-two years with the E. W. Scripps Company, retiring in 2010 after serving twelve years as vice president and general manager of WCPO-TV. He lives in Cincinnati with his wife, Sally, two children and their families which include three grandchildren.